T0380815

Attitude of Gratitude

IN SERVICE TO THE LIGHT BOOK TWO

Written by Archangel Michael
Transcribed by Michele D. Baker

BALBOA.PRESS
A DIVISION OF HAY HOUSE

Balboa Press books may be ordered through booksellers or by contacting:

Balboa Press
A Division of Hay House
1663 Liberty Drive
Bloomington, IN 47403
www.balboapress.com
844-682-1282

Because of the dynamic nature of the Internet, any web addresses or links contained in this book may have changed since publication and may no longer be valid. The views expressed in this work are solely those of the author and do not necessarily reflect the views of the publisher, and the publisher hereby disclaims any responsibility for them.

The author of this book does not dispense medical advice or prescribe the use of any technique as a form of treatment for physical, emotional, or medical problems without the advice of a physician, either directly or indirectly. The intent of the author is only to offer information of a general nature to help you in your quest for emotional and spiritual well-being. In the event you use any of the information in this book for yourself, which is your constitutional right, the author and the publisher assume no responsibility for your actions.

Any people depicted in stock imagery provided by Getty Images are models, and such images are being used for illustrative purposes only.
Certain stock imagery © Getty Images.

Print information available on the last page.

ISBN: 979-8-7652-4235-3 (sc)
ISBN: 979-8-7652-4239-1 (e)

Library of Congress Control Number: 2023909640

Balboa Press rev. date: 07/31/2023

For my grandmothers

Evelyn Louise Weinreich Saathoff
& Margaret Irene Strang Baker Hoffman

who taught me about gratitude

"Be still and in gratitude
and simply allow."
        - Archangel Michael

FOREWORD

by Mike Dooley

Of all places... I found Michele Baker's first book, *All We Need Is Love,* on a bookshelf in my home office during the latter days of the COVID sequestration. How it got there is still a mystery, though it's clear the timing was perfect. This student was ready, and the teacher appeared. As I read, it offered exciting ideas that confirmed my own evolving understandings on the nature of reality, while new insights abounded. Shocked and awed by this discovery, I wrote to Michele with gratitude, and she replied.

As if she hadn't given me enough already, I'm one of the very few people who've received an advance copy of her second book, *Attitude of Gratitude,* now in your hands. No surprise, it's perfect for the next steps in my own journey, and I strongly suspect it will have the same relevance in yours. Herein, you will find a magical blend of profound and inspiring words, interspersed with the candid musings and struggles of the author. I can relate; I think all of us can. In some cases, Michele unabashedly shares with her spirit guides and readers her own challenges and self-doubts, while in others she allows us to connect these dots for ourselves. Such humble transparency, coupled with the loving cajoling words she channels, is a fabulous reminder that life is indeed an adventure and that none of us are here to go it alone—by design we walk our paths with unknown friends and supportive guides.

These are unusual times we're living through, making the guidance you'll find within most timely. It was no more by chance that you found *your* copy of this book, than the relevance its words will have on your unique life. You're ready for it. And in one way or another, you made this happen. Her guides speak of the presently rising vibrations and energies of the planet, sharing that we're about to leave behind our primitive understandings of spirituality, survival, and thriving. There's a new world order stirring for fellow, like-minded thinkers and readers; heaven on earth awaits. Actually, it's been here all along, we've just needed to learn how to see it. With the help of this book, those who have found it, or vice versa, will soon have brand-new realizations concerning life's majesty and their own power. Simultaneously, they'll begin to possess an ever-increasing awareness of humanity's oneness. To realize the importance of cooperation, even with those they disagree with, and respect for all. And then finally, you'll begin to recognize and use the supernatural gifts that all of us are endowed with, to live consciously, intentionally, with purpose and in love.

We all chose to be here at this exciting time when everyone would have the opportunity to transform *themselves* into the angel-like beings we truly are. In the very near future, within this very lifetime, we'll soon be so much further along than we are today that we'll look back at our former selves in utter disbelief, wondering how it could have ever been so difficult to surrender to life's grace and be carried along by the unfailing winds of a loving Universe. With Michele's guides, you'll become aware of our own, phenomenally creative power to live in ease, infallibly guided by spirit—your own. You've nearly made it. Not to the end, but to the beginning of further adventures unimaginable. Key tipping points have already been reached, you paid your dues a long time ago, and enlightenment beckons. The rest of your life is about to become the best of your life, the payback you were born deserving.

Yours in the adventure,
Mike Dooley
NY Times bestselling author of *Infinite Possibilities*
and creator of *Notes from the Universe*

"Simply expressing gratitude may have lasting effects on the brain."
    – Dr. Wong and Dr. Brown

INTRODUCTION (OR, "HOW TO USE THIS BOOK") REDUX

Before you buy this book, you should know a few things.

First, I stole this introduction from Book One (well, "borrowed"), because when I went back to rewrite this section, I found I had already said everything I wanted to say in the first book's introduction, and as I am a huge believer in not reinventing the wheel (and it was mine to begin with), I decided to adapt it. Long story short, you may have seen this before if you read Book One (which I hope you have)!

Second, I believe in reincarnation and past lives (and lives taking place in other simultaneous dimensions, too). I believe there are numerous other sentient beings in our Universe, and some of those other beings have already visited Earth and are even here now.

Finally, I hear Angels – usually Archangel Michael, but lately also Archangel Gabriel and a whole host of other extra-dimensional beings: I think of them as "My Team" – and I write down in my journal what They say.

The book you hold in your hands is an almost-verbatim transcript of these journals. The entries I left out were the completely personal messages which simply were not relevant to anyone but me or which made no sense in context now that Book One is published and available on Amazon and Balboa Press.com (yes, a shameless plug for Book One, now available in softcover, e-Book, and audiobook versions).

I changed the names of the people My Team talks about, so they will not be embarrassed, except for my friend Lelon, who gave permission to leave his name intact. Other than that, these pages contain much of what I have used the automatic writing process to put down. You are watching me go through the process of Ascension, as you will soon go (or already going!) through it yourself. I suggest you skim through this book and find passages to read – they are in chronological order, so start anywhere. Flip through the book and let intuition stop you on the page you need to see that day. In most cases, the material does not build on previous material (except in a few cases, which is why I have included an index and a glossary), so you can read this book out of order, from front to back, or sporadically. There is also an all-new Additional Reading section, and I strongly urge you to do more digging on your own.

Remember, too, that My Team has a sense of humor, and They often laugh *with* me, and *at* me. I simply write down what I hear, so you may see "(laughter)," which means my Team just said something that They found funny, or delightful; or They are happy; or perhaps I just thought something that They considered ridiculous, and They responded to that by laughing incredulously.

A lot of what I write is new to me – I do not really know or understand what I've written until I go back and read it afterward, and some of it seems a little "out there," but when I go back, it all feels real, and True, so what the heck... just go with it. I invite you to use your own discernment when you read this book. Read it and *feel* it – use your first instinct, your gut feelings. In other words, take from this book what resonates with you. I hope that these first words resonate with you and inspire you to realize the Truth: you are nothing less than a Divine Spark temporarily residing inside a human body, and your Divine birthright is to co-create and have an amazing experience. It is all there, and it's all true.

I have said it before, but it bears repeating: I am just a regular person like you, just with this mission to be in the front wave, so others can look and see what is coming at the top of the next hill. In that spirit, I still offer myself and hope the lessons, revelations – and occasional mishaps – are of use to you on this journey we are all on together.

Every day, I hope something reminds you to be grateful for the beauty in your life!

Michele D. Baker
P.S. I don't have writer's block anymore.

"Gratitude is the sign of noble souls."
– Aesop

Michele D. Baker

MAY 12, 2016
HOME

Archangel Michael:

We are glad to see and feel your delight, Beloved One. We told you to make this simple change to help you see the real effects of following the path — it can be a pleasant stroll through the woods or a hard slog up a rocky pathway. Either way will get you to where you are going, but some ways are more enjoyable than others! As always, your free will allows you to choose. (Remember, too, that your free will also allows you to choose again.)

Sleep now, and we will speak in the morning early. You have a download and an upgrade scheduled for tonight, but We will ensure you sleep well and wake up rested. Pleasant evening to you!

MAY 13, 2016
HOME

Archangel Michael:

Today We wish to explain about the fractal nature of the Universe. This is Archangel Gabriel's favorite topic as music and communication are fractal, too — so I, the Blessed Archangel Michael, will yield to my friend and companion, Archangel Gabriel.

Archangel Gabriel:

So, little one, now We may speak as a thousand suns touch their fleeting rays on the pebbles of a thousand beaches. (laughter) It is true that my choice of speech as you perceive it is much more flowery than that of Archangel Michael. He is a straightforward "speaker," whereas I enjoy the beauty of language; like music, it pours from my tongue like raindrops upon parched land. There I go again! (more laughter)

You have heard before the saying "as above, so below," and this is literally true. The Universe is a magnificent sphere of Oneness and embodies the soulful essence of sacred geometry (see Book One for more details), best represented by a fractal. The tiniest leaf contains small triangular edges that themselves mirror the shape of the leaf; the tree mirrors the same shape when seen from afar, and the tree mimics the wedge shape of the forest. This is but a simple example, Beloved, but one that holds true across the vast spectrum of the luminous Universe. Every delicate part is a shadow of a larger whole and is in itself mirrored by the tiny nature of its substructural parts and cellular magnificence.

But why are we telling you this? Because, like a beautiful but complicated musical composition made from a gentle melody, a vibrant harmony, high ringing notes and foundations of bass, the Universe vibrates thusly, too. Displace but a single phrase or note and the whole is diminished. But in every moment, every Now, there is the opportunity to "get back on key" and return the pleasing composition to the ear. This is joyous news, Beloved! For when you "fail" – which of course never actually happens – in but the space of a heartbeat there is room and opportunity for redemption, and in every Now, every second, every heartbeat, the Universe completely realigns itself to meet the needs of the whole. Just as Gaia lives a breathes, so too does the vast web of the tenebrous Universe, breathing and respiring a gentle resonance that binds the whole together.

A fractal Universe allows and commands every creature within it to constantly _be_, to add to the sum that is greater than the whole of the parts. It also allows for unparalleled flexibility to grow, change, blossom, wither, die, recall, begin, end…

Archangel Michael:

Basically, you cannot go wrong, as the Universe is self-correcting.

Archangel Gabriel:

Yes, that concept applies. The beings have at once free will to err and the comfort of knowing that a solution to any problem is imminent.

Archangel Michael:

We are so glad to speak with you today, Beloved. Rest now and we will say more later.

MAY 14, 2016
HOME

Archangel Michael:

Yes, Beloved, this book [*The War of Art,* by Steven Pressman] has much to teach you about resistance. This is the mysterious mountain you have been climbing around for years, and the very thing [your friend and spiritual mentor] Lelon and your mother spoke of. Indeed, Our Frank[1] was divinely inspired to lead you to this book to impart the lesson that you are not alone, to dismiss your idea that you don't have enough willpower (you do!) and that as you "turn pro" as Pressman would say, you are learning to be at one with your Mission. Of course, Beloved, this writer comes from a place of war, the masculine need to fight and argue and dominate. This author is a "do-er," not a "be-er," but he is a product of his way, and of the 3D plane on which he lives. This is good and works well but you will never be this, Dearest. Your Mission is to transcend that level of thinking and being and create from a place of pure joy! This is no hardship, but a magical and fruitful partnership between the seemingly different celestial realms and the Earth plane. Of course, you hear Us laughing at the notion that it could be separate; it is not now and ever was, but the human consciousness has not yet collectively reached a point where the absolute connection is readily apparent. That time is coming soon. Meanwhile, keep writing – you need to speak with Us! – and continue to transcribe the other notes. Things are moving quickly now. We love you and We will speak again soon.

MAY 15, 2016

Archangel Michael:

Good evening, Beloved! Although you do not realize it, today was a day of great growth and change for you. We did indeed do some work while you were on the road to Nashville, which you experienced as "time warps" or "time out of time." Also, although you do not remember it, We bilocated you and your vehicle at one point when another car came suddenly into your lane (no, not when you honked at the driver for pulling in too closely) – this was in Alabama in heavy traffic. You do not even know it occurred, and neither does the other driver (we "moved" him, too). The next few days will be great learning times and tools for you so try to enjoy yourself. We will help you!

And yes, We heard and acknowledge your command to quit eating sugar. This one action will have far-reaching consequences for you physically and mentally: sugar is – as your aunt said – a metabolic poison, lovely though it tastes. We will take away the urge, but you must do the work. Sleep well, Princess; We will speak with you again tomorrow.

---

[1] Author's note: when my guides speak of someone they placed in my path to help me understand a concept or issue, they often refer to that person as "Our" [Person's First Name] to distinguish between the relationship I have with that person on a normal friendship or family level and their role as a connector to a specific piece of knowledge. In this case, my friend Frank recommended *The War of Art* which was important for me to read, so at that time, he was acting as a conduit of information for my Team, thus temporarily becoming "[Their]" Frank.

Gratitude Game #1

GROUND/CENTER/SHIELD

GROUND yourself by saying out loud: *"I feel the roots from deep in the Earth, branching up through my feet, anchoring me to the Earth and the limitless power in it. I feel the roots coming up through my feet, my legs, into my back, going down my arms and into my hands, up my neck and into my head, connecting me to the boundless power in the Earth. I am connected to all things."*

CENTER yourself by placing your hands below your belly button (your "hara" or sacral chakra) and saying: *"I feel the awareness that normally lives behind my eyes dropping down, past my mouth, past my neck, past my chest, past my stomach, and settling just below my belly button. Here, my awareness is in the exact center of my body, and I can move in any direction with perfect balance."*

SHIELD yourself by saying out loud: *"I feel a warm, clear liquid cascading over my head, enveloping me in a warm, clear shield that bounces out negativity and lets in only what I invite in. I feel it covering my head, my face, my neck, my chest, my back, my arms, my hands, my stomach, my legs, my feet. I am perfectly protected."*

Michele D. Baker

MAY 16, 2016
NASHVILLE, TENNESSEE

Archangel Michael:

Most brilliant morning to you, Beloved! We know your rest was interrupted but We also used the opportunity to access a lesson in compassion; one which you had wished for but had not had the time yet to "do." This was indeed a good night for you, with an upgrade that was only possible because you have moved to a place beyond sugar. You will notice many changes now, so be on the lookout for signposts!

LATER THAT DAY

Archangel Michael:

All flows in Divine Right Order and in Divine Right Timing. Already today you see the potential for cooperation as loving beings come together harmoniously to celebrate their children. As never before, there are parents watching over their children's welfare and allowing them to develop into very rounded adults. Although they are scripted and pampered, there can be no doubt that these children – many of whom came in "prepackaged" to know languages and music and mathematics – are very loved. They have arrived on a plane that now values children and cares for them as never before.

We wish to speak more of bilocation and your increased ability to do this very normal activity. There is nothing else you must do or learn to accomplish this; indeed, the decision to reduce or eliminate sugar was the final "roadblock" to your consciously committing an act of bilocation. We will give you more details very soon. Until then, see how much fresher and clearer your skin tone appears, and how much clearer your mind? We will speak again.

MAY 17, 2016
NASHVILLE, TENNESSEE

Archangel Michael:

Do not judge, nor be so quick to make assumptions, Beloved. The humans at this level are doing all they can to be good people. They try very hard: they make the "right money," send their children to the "best" schools, ensure they play sports and learn a musical instrument, attend church, and grow to love gadgets and designer shoes. They are all products of their environments, but they do not yet fully comprehend the wider world around them. They do not yet realize that they are asleep – they have good intentions, and yes, that is admirable. They will awaken soon, for their children already embody the new way. They play together in harmony with others who are not like themselves; they follow an example of love without prompting; they forgive easily and often, creating community effortlessly wherever they are. They will be good examples for their parents!

These are profound lessons for you, Beloved – to come upon a group of people who look like you yet do not think, feel, or react like you! Judgement is a useless exercise (you know this) as each individual serves his or her own spiritual growth and development in his own Divine Right Timing. The spiral always moves up; it just moves at different speeds.

In a similar vein, We call your attention to your friend's parents. They, too, are products of their environment and circumstances. The healing occurring in that family is coming fast and hard as they band together in support of the patriarch's illness. Indeed, this one event has created a more loving family unit than ever before. These lovely humans are living more than ever moment by moment, a wonderful reminder for you to do the same.

We feel your arrogance, hubris, and pride, Beloved, and caution you not to judge; again, We say *do not judge*. Discernment is wise, but judgement is merely lazy thinking. You can – and have done – better. We love you as the unique and special celestial being you are, so go and rest. We will speak again soon.

MAY 18, 2016
NASHVILLE, TENNESSEE

Archangel Michael:

So many young and powerful beings of the Light are in your sphere of influence now! These children in school now are as loving and caring as they are wise. The few who choose to prey upon others are fulfilling their contracts to act as the adversary (for contrast) and they, too, are doing their jobs admirably. Soon there will be no more need for this kind of contrast – every person will have the things he or she needs and will flourish into the fullest expression of Divine Light: the poets, the artists, the musicians, the healers, the adventurers – each will have the needed attention and skills to complete his chosen mission. We also say that every young hue-man (not just in the chronological sense) goes through this phase of "misbehavior" – how else could one learn? This is precisely why Earth school is set in such density; it is a buffer between practicing humans and the rest of Galactic civilization. When beings first learn to "use their powers" things can be messy (laughter), so 3D acts as a giant drop cloth to catch the spills!

This is all We wish to say now, but please come back to us before bed.

LATER THAT DAY

Archangel Michael:

Things are becoming clearer now, our Beloved One. Can you see them? Can you feel them? Can you sense the tide moving swiftly all around you, yet you are wrapped in a bubble of calm collectedness? Such is it to live always in the Now. The world swirls around, yet you remain "separate" from it, seeing and experiencing all, and one with it, but not *of* it. This mental clarity is one result of the spiritual clarity caused by an increased physical clarity. The one best thing you have done for your spiritual well-being was to largely eliminate sugar from your diet. As "time passes" (yes, We feel how funny that sounds) your cravings for many things will decrease, including all processed foods, meat, dairy and even grains. You will actively seek out a plant-based diet. This first step is a good one, Beloved, and with it you will travel even faster than before – all is coming into Divine Right Timing. The way is paved for miracles now!

Rest now. We love you so much! There is a download coming tonight, but it will be gentle, so have no fear.

MAY 19, 2016
NASHVILLE, TENNESSEE

Archangel Michael:

Good morning, Angel being! We did indeed give you an upgrade in the night and that's why you had to get up twice to go to the bathroom; downloads and upgrades flush toxins from your system as they integrate. The 3D body (now a 5D body) is amazing technology, Beloved – always respect it. Your task is to "create Heaven on Earth" so that means being in the body and appreciating it. Your particular body is becoming increasingly special as the extra senses and gifts come online. You are to be a model for others of how the body can heal, change form, move from place to place, act as a communication device over long distances, etc. These seem wondrous, but they are not, Beloved. Every galactic being has these abilities and very soon, many Earth hue-mans will, too. Feel today the lightness of spirit that comes with being at peace in your physical "vehicle." Enjoy your day and We will speak to you again soon!

Yes, you may eat pancakes for breakfast!

MAY 20, 2016
HOME

Archangel Michael:

We send you this song ("Am I Wrong" by Nico & Vinz) as an example of a song/art/ infusion of the new order and variety. The catchy tune and the inspired lyrics create a song of lasting power and worth. And no, he's not "wrong." (laughter)

There is much to discuss today, Beloved, but little time now. Please come to us later and leave an hour of your earth time. Enjoy the day!

LATER THAT DAY

Archangel Michael:

We wish to speak this evening of the book you shall produce. The conversation you had with Our Frank was most helpful, but you will find that your experience will be much different, Beloved One. There will be very little editing beyond that required for the layperson's general understanding. We will guide the editor and she (yes, a "she") will see the wisdom behind the words. The book shall bear your name on the cover, but in the foreword, you will explain Our process – We speak and you record, using your wisdom and experience to pull the words and sentences into being. This is the way of a Channel, although We prefer the term Vessel (We know that you do not, beloved). To Our eyes, a Vessel is complete and filled with the purpose of the Mission. Then it spills over onto the Earth. This is a very clear image – a beautiful pot overflowing with cool, clear water. We sense that you prefer Channel, although that word also feels inadequate. It is a pure stream from another realm, but you Beloved, are most definitely participating! We read your mood and thoughts, and use your memories and experiences to choose words and images from the thousands of choices available... To make sure the message is clear, concise, beautiful and understandable. Without your grounding on Earth, we could not frame our thoughts in a way that 3D humans would recognize. So while the Channel is a pure stream, it is a shared stream; and, as you know, sometimes your questions and thoughts frame what We have to say or which direction a conversation should go. So this book is imminent, beloved. The time has come to present your typed version to a publisher. Part of your vacation job is to finish typing the two books' messages. After that, things will move so quickly that you will scarcely know what end is up! But you have always been at your best when there is much going on.

We also want to tell you and confirm that the book is but one step in this mission. There will be speeches and lessons as well. But as you enjoy talking to groups, this will be a fun activity and not at all a burden to you. There may be a way to have Lelon do a platform medium reading at these as well. "Messages from the other side."

There is much to do. Devote some time each day to transcribing the previous messages, now and in the coming weeks. The hour approaches that you have waited for, beloved Earth Angel. This is what you've been waiting for!

On the topic of bilocation, we cannot of course give you a specific date, for several reasons – such as "time doesn't exist," and "the potentials don't discriminate that finely" – but We feel it will be soon. Enjoy your last days of traveling by car!

We are so proud of you for taking up this mission; now rest and begin again tomorrow.

MAY 22, 2016
AM, HOME

Archangel Michael:

Ah, Beloved, We hear the interesting questions in your head from last night's discussion, which was wonderful to Us – to hear hue-mans exercising their brains and intellect and using discernment rather than simply regurgitating facts. This is a blessing!

As to the question of whether Gaia is round or flat, that is a very interesting discussion. Let us proceed.

In a strictly 3D sense – which doesn't exist anymore, as the 3D Earth plane, the one in which humans were all two-strand beings, ceased to exist when 4D took its place in 2012 – the Earth, as most beings perceived it, is a sphere, a ball of rock hurtling through space and time. The 4D Earth, whose celestial body and Soul are the entity or being called Gaia, is none of the shapes you would recognize. Seen from a great distance, your Earth or Gaia would appear as a gaseous mass in space, like a cloud perhaps. There is no longer a solid form for Earth, and the fact that humans portray planets and stars as balls of gas and rock is due to an accident in perception, much like the way your senses perceive time as linear, or your eyes perceive a vanishing point on the horizon. Of course, it is not there – the perception of a vanishing point is due solely to one point of reference,

Michele D. Baker

and when you move, *it* moves. There is also the popular notion that a sphere is the most efficient configuration in creation, and indeed, something close to this is correct. We have spoken before of sacred geometry and how a point becomes a line and how many points become a sphere. Thus is all creation formed: from a single point with movement, a perfect balance of stillness and movement, Yin and Yang, dot and line. As to how this relates to the Earth's physical body, the Earth is a hollow ball, and the objects on the planet (which is spherical, but not a perfect sphere), stay on its surface because of gravity. Gravity is not created, however, by the core of your planet, but rather by another celestial law that does work. (More on gravity later.)

In some ways, 3D (or two-DNA-strand) humans are like children. They observe everything but create false or incorrect interpretations for their explanations, mostly out of ignorance. This is not to say that humans are ignorant; but if a person is not yet sufficiently awakened to know other ways, other alternatives, then those explanations will reach deaf ears. Your guide Archimedes wishes to say something here.

Archimedes:

It is a profound pleasure to speak with you as a being of light in service to our shared planet, Gaia! I applaud you for your willingness and ability to complete the Herculean task set before you. This is indeed worthy of praise and salutations. As a master architect and member of the Galactic Creation League, I wish to shed light on this topic of Earth and her creation. The same can be applied to all planetary bodies that choose to exist in an incarnated state; that is, you may take this lesson and apply it to other systems and stars in our Universe.

In the beginning, We came together to create planets upon which beings could incarnate, as there are some lessons or experiences or menu items (delighted laughter) that are best (and only!) able to occur while in a flesh-and-blood body. Planets were created in the forms requested by each Soul – Gaia chose a near perfect sphere with much water, some land, and the correct distance from the Sun to permit a fragile ecosystem of animal and plant life. This physical planet was manifested in the same way that all items, things, planets – *everything!* – is manifested: with a shared vision of the desired outcome, Gaia sprang forth from the Heavens. This is not to say that the Earth sprang forth from *nothing*. As you know, energy can neither be created nor destroyed, as balance must be maintained. Rather, the Universe moved to create the Earth, and it was.

As for the physical shape, the Earth 3D body is an irregular sphere, as that shape produces the intended effects Gaia requested, such as seasons and weather, which would not be possible unless rotation occurred. The tilt of the planet is also intentional, as it allows for temperature regulation, and therefore, seasons.

The moon – ah, *la bella Luna* – *la dama Luna* – She is a marvelous machine put into orbit around your planet as a metallic planetoid waystation for visitors from other galaxies. Yes, the Moon is a bustling place, filled with visitors! The reason you cannot see them is because they are on different frequencies: 5D and higher, or the "notes" between the black and white keys on a piano. There is a simple way to explain this information you've already assimilated.

We have explained to you that bilocation (the correct term for teleportation) is like stepping up, then over and then back down. OK, now imagine you step "up" and "over," but instead of coming down, you simply hang out in the "over." This is where those visiting beings are: in the "over."

The Moon is a metallic planetoid whose purpose is to provide a resting place for incarnate visitors who wish to visit Earth. Kind of like a hotel, except that the beds are always clean and soft, and the television gets a lot more channels! (much laughter)

Archangel Michael:

Thank you, my dear Archimedes. We must speak some more on this topic, but for now We feel Vessel is wearying; her hand needs a break. Come back later and We will speak again.

LATER:

Archimedes:

Thank you, Blessed Archangel Michael. I will finish the lesson now.

Planets of all kinds are created in the same way. It is much the same as when an egg cell divides to create a human embryo. First, there is a single point of energy in "space." The point of energy moves (in any direction, it does not matter which) and then stops. Now there are two points with a line between them; movement has occurred. Each point is now connected to the other by the imaginary line between them. This is a simple idea which anyone can understand.

Now, imagine that from that source point, countless lines race out simultaneously in all directions and stop – you now have a hollow sphere. Millions and millions of imaginary lines, each connecting the source point to another point in space. Do you see the connection to a cell, a thin wall surrounding a hollow center? This is the first movement in all directions, and the first sphere.

Now the process repeats. From one of the points on the "surface" of the sphere, millions of lines race outward and stop; now there are two spheres. One becomes two. Two become four, four become eight, and so it goes until an entire planet is formed.

"Part of gratitude is reaching out to say *Hello, I love you today.*"
- Archangel Michael

Michele D. Baker

This "magic" happens in the blink of an eye, and it can be used to create human cells, leaves, rocks, or even planets. Once the planet has reached its desired incarnation, the process slows down and balance is achieved. The "cells" constantly renew, and as old cells die, others are birthed to take their places.

LATER:

Archangel Michael:

Hello, Beloved and good evening to you! We know all the work you are doing for Us on the 3D/5D plane, and We wish to thank you for it and the many times you tried to explain what We had in Our collective minds – your knowledge of language and customs to help audiences understand and engage with the books is invaluable to Us and makes us true partners in bringing these Messages to Earth. Merely by listening and recording you are doing a great service and fulfilling your Mission.

We hear in your mind that you wish to know more about gravity. We will oblige and add that material here. Archimedes wishes to speak again now.

Archimedes:

Greetings from Archimedes, Master of Mathematics and Architecture on the 3D plane of your ancient Greece. Tonight, I wish to bring you additional information about the Universal law known here on Earth as "gravity." Because this exists on other planets as well, I will give general information on those planets and then specifically on Earth's gravitational field.

"Modern" humans believe they exist at the apex of literacy and scientific knowledge, but this is not the case. (In fact, much has been lost and current humans actually know less as a species than in "primitive civilizations" such as Egypt, Greece, Incan, Mayan, etc.) In my time in Greece, we knew about astronomy, astrology, geology, metallurgy, biology, physics, chemistry and more. We knew the stars were distant suns whose light took billions of years to reach us, and we knew much about the other planets in our solar system and in our galaxy. We knew of Pluto long ago and its movements in relationship to the movements and objects of the other planets in this system. We knew that the kind of life on Earth could not exist on other planets because of the chemical makeup of those incarnations (bodies) and because of the electromagnetic frequencies of those planets, which are different from those on Earth. The way these 3D human bodies are constructed, they could not exist in the much-denser gravity – not to mention the unbreathable atmosphere – of some of the other planets nearby, like Mars and Venus.

The gravity produced by the physical planet Earth is very special: the electromagnetic force of this planet is exactly correct to allow humans to exist here and flourish. Gravity, however, is not a product of a molten core as it is on planets closer to the sun, specifically Venus. In fact, your planet has a molten layer higher up than most planets, and the Earth's crust floats on this like the skin of an orange, tethered lightly and sporadically by a membrane touching this molten layer. There is then a hollow space where beings exist. Thus, the "hollow Earth" theory is partially correct; the Earth's very center is a large solid mass of metal, the magnetic mass of which pulls everything inward. This also explains why the Earth is a slightly flattened sphere and not a perfect one, and why there is a tilt – the core is a slight disk so there is more pull in some places than in others.

Archangel Michael:

We feel your deep skepticism, Beloved, let Us come to you tomorrow and make this clear.

LATER:

Archangel Michael:

Good evening, Beloved. We are so glad to hear your voice in Our minds this beautiful evening! There is so much to tell, We have a hard time knowing where to begin.

First, thank you for coming to Us tonight – We feel your low energy and your exhaustion, and We therefore very much appreciate you writing first before sleeping.

Next, we wish to finish the section on gravity – there is one last piece We wish you to include, so please take this information and insert that into its proper location.

Archangel Michael and Archimedes:

Regarding gravity, we have explained that the Earth has a hollow space and that the center is not molten, but rather a solid spherical metal or mass. This mass is critical to gravity as it contains elements that interact together to form a magnetic force (electromagnetic) that assists in gravity. The mass – we shall simply say "the core" from now on – is a combination of metals that have magnetic properties. The force fields of energy (Merkabas) around every living thing are also magnetic in nature. (This allows animals such as birds and fish to move from place to place hundreds or thousands of miles away and then return to the original location; they are navigating using the magnetic properties of their Merkabas.) Some people's energy is more strongly electromagnetic. But all living things generate a magnetic force in some amount and frequency, and as like

Michele D. Baker

Gratitude Game #2

17-SECOND INTENTIONS

SET THE INTENTION for your day when you wake up by taking just 17 seconds to make a roadmap for the Universe to follow.

It might go something like this:

"Today I see the beauty in all my interactions and relationships. I accomplish A, B, and C and notice how effortless it is to be present in the moment and how easy it is to get things done when I simply allow the Universe to take care of me."

(Note that your intention is in the present tense - the "Now" - and spoken as if it has already real.)

Clap your hands three times and blow yourself a kiss.

Michele D. Baker

attracts like, those individual fields are attracted to the core of Gaia/Earth. (Incidentally, remember that all things on Earth are alive, Beloved. You know this: rocks, plants, water, animals – everything is alive and interacting with its environment, including the planet itself.) Thus, you have "gravity," which in Truth is the Universal law of "like attracts like" at work, in the form of magnetic fields interacting with each other.

On a side note, it is interesting that magnetic fields of course come in many gradations of intensity, and again, "like attracts like," so some people, or places, or things seem more familiar or comfortable as they are closer in frequency to your own native frequency. (It's why you have so much furniture made of solid wood in your home, Beloved and hardly any metal. You resonate strongly with the electromagnetic frequency of trees.)[2]

These magnetic fields, the natural electricity in your atmosphere – think static electricity, electric current and lightning – form electromagnetic fields as well, and without these interactions, many of your systems would not exist. Think of the example of a cellphone demagnetizing the magnetic strip on your credit card or hotel room key. Think of a large magnet erasing computer data on an old VHS tape. Remember, your body is also like a huge computer – these forces influence it and can change the human body as it currently exists in 3D/4D "reality." (Ask yourself why people die when struck by lightning or when "criminals" are electrocuted.)

There is lesser damage done to the body during magnetic resonance imaging (MRI), although the magnets do interfere with the body's ability to maintain a stable magnetic field (Merkaba). It's also why many are protesting the advent of 5G internet technology – the electrical current is not beneficial to the human body (or to other species' bodies). However, with an MRI, the magnetic field or Merkaba can withstand short bursts before memory is affected or the cells begin to break down, and some humans are nearer in frequency to the "key" used by the MRI machine, and therefore face fewer side effects.

We know you are fascinated by this unexpected puzzle piece dropping into place but sleep now. We can talk more tomorrow. Good night!

---

[2] The study of these connections is part of the Chinese Five Element Theory (wood, water, metal, fire, water). There are also connections to Feng Shui, which seeks to control the flow of energy (qi/chi/ki) based on building design and the strategic placement of objects. For more, see Appendix C.

Archangel Michael:

We are so pleased that you received Our gift – the offer of transcription from Jeff. You know it was right, Beloved and indeed, all will go much quicker with this task divided in half.

Things move very quickly now. Spend some time typing the previous messages, so the full book will be ready. The world needs a book written by a "regular" woman, Beloved, and this gift is for them. We rejoice in that, and indeed move the Universe to bring its creation into the physical plane. All will come in good time, but the next step is close. Watch for the publisher that literally drops in your lap. The marketing materials you have begun receiving via email will be of use as well, although others will fall into place to handle much of this for you. We will not ask you to do any task which does not delight or empower you. For there are those who delight in the sharing of information, and there are those (like you) who do not. We know that you prefer to create the product but not to send it out, and so we will provide someone to love that task for you in your place.

Yes, you had a short download this afternoon; this is why you were dizzy and nauseated. The DNA is reconfiguring so fast, your 3D/4D self sometimes cannot assimilate fast enough. Internal changes are occurring: your blood chemistry is changing and soon the "switchover" will be complete. The crystalline matrix, which is the birthright of humans, and which allows humans to become hue-mans, is manifesting within your cells at an ever-increasing rate. The cells convert from their regular RNA to C-RNA and the new configuration will allow for instantaneous changes, including regrowing limbs or skin or organs, reorganization into another equivalent format (from blonde to brunette, or 2 inches taller, for example), or the ability to phase in and out of what seems to be "normal" space-time. Yes, this is the longed-for teleportation! It is no coincidence that you've been watching [the television show] Heroes; the gifts presented on the show are some of the common gifts that will become the new normal. Hearing thoughts, flying, teleportation, regeneration, shapeshifting... On a 4D/5D plane, these are very ordinary, Beloved and not at all unusual. Soon, every human will become a hue-man, and these gifts will manifest across a wide spectrum.

So, the ever-present question from Our beloved Vessel: *When?* Soon! The potentials align and manifestation approaches. Meanwhile, enjoy the last vestiges of the old way. We love you so much; come back tomorrow and We will speak again.

Archangel Michael:

Thank you, Beloved, for going to sleep last night when We asked you to – you had a special upgrade in the night, which is why you slept so restlessly and kept waking up. We do apologize, but this was so critical, it simply could not wait or be otherwise. The upgrade will manifest over the next days, so watch for some radical changes in your eating habits and in the quality of your skin – these will be the most obvious outward signs that the process is almost complete.

Were you to measure the rate of change over of your DNA, you would see an exponential increase in the cellular conversion. What is happening now is that the DNA is literally changing from one form to another form – a crystalline structure that is all but impervious to disease, wear, strain, breakage and harm. This structure is light enough in vibration to permit complete dematerialization, meaning you can completely reorganize your physical shell in any way you wish at the molecular level. Of course, your old DNA changed at the molecular level, too, but not at the rate of speed soon possible.

Since crystalline DNA is not underpinned by genes, no traits from your parents (brown eyes, short waist, soft hair…) will have to be kept, although of course you may *choose* to keep your hereditary markers that proclaim you a member of your family group. It does mean that if you wish to suddenly have blue eyes, or be 12 inches taller, it is possible in the blink of an eye!

These changes are really very ordinary, Beloved, as a fixed, immutable body is a rarity and only possible within the low density of 3D. In other realms and on other planes, the physical shells are simply upgraded, modified or repaired – never buried or burned after just one use. From our perspective, and without judgment, to a viewer from our level, the cremation of a body at the end of life would be like burning a beautiful coat after wearing it only once.

The physical vehicle you now inhabit has a much longer "shelf life" than even the relatively-heavy 3D plane should be able to exhaust. The bodies around you decay too quickly because of environmental toxins, poor diet and hygiene, and because they are assumed to wear out after only 80 years. Nothing could be further from the truth, Beloved! Your physical bodies, even with only two strands of DNA, should last hundreds of years. The fact that they do not is a testament to the power of the Dark, which has brainwashed humans into believing that a 75 year life span is normal. But you must understand – no amount of brainwashing would ever have succeeded unless *humans went along with it*. This is a free will Universe that bends and moves to meet the wishes and desires created by the beings in it. Thus, if a human chooses to inhabit a sick and decaying body for only 75 years, the Universe will honor that wish as the command that it is.

So we hear your question - what about those souls whose contracts call for illness? Yes, Beloved, these do exist, and those cases are honored to teach Soul level lessons. But truly, some Souls simply choose to be ill, for they seem to need the attention devoted to the sick. Or they misinterpret download symptoms and mentally invent an illness which they then manifest. Remember, Beloved, this is all without judgment; each is creating his or her own unique existence.

We feel your hand cramping, so good night.

MAY 27, 2016
AM, HOME

Archangel Michael:

We wish to immediately continue where we left off yesterday, Beloved. Regarding "illness," there is so much more to say!

The human body as it exists in a two-strand connected state is indeed vulnerable – We might even say "prone to" – physical illness and disease (dis-ease). We make a distinction here because "illness" is caused by external forces – you cut yourself and it becomes infected – and "disease" is caused by internal thoughts, feelings, suppressed emotions ("I *think* I am sick, therefore I *am* sick") or simple creation of a desired outcome (the Universe moves to fulfill your unspoken or unconscious desire to be sick). It is true that once your 3D body (in this case we use 3D as synonymous with "two strand") becomes sick, it can be much more difficult to "climb up out of the pit" to become well again.

Let us take a simple example. A child experiences a download during which she has flu-like symptoms which are mistaken for flu. Her mother keeps her home from school to rest, and naturally once the download has finished "processing" a few days later, the child is again well. In reality, there was never any flu, but the outcome – the need for bed rest – was the same, so the symptoms manifested in a way so as to produce the needed result. In truth, this was never really "illness," only a need for rest to ease the transition of the download.

Another example: chronic sufferers of stomach ailments (almost all types) are often denying themselves the "spiritual nutrition" available to them. Perhaps they are naturally fearful people, or they have experienced terrorizing influences, or they worry about money, children, jobs or spouses to excess. Their stomachs are "tied in knots" both metaphorically and literally, and they experience the associated symptoms of stomach

Gratitude Game #3

LEMONS → LEMONADE

Turn your daily "lemons" into "lemonade."

My day job is so boring!
I hate going to dumb meetings.

→

I am so grateful that I have a job that allows me to earn a fair wage in a comfy, air-conditioned office.

_____

→

_____

→

_____

→

Michele D. Baker

problems. A related issue is the growing disconnect between the world a person lives in and the world she wishes to inhabit (a happier, more just, kind, clean world, for example). As the gap between the two widens, "dis-ease" results. Because humans are largely products of their environments, and because those environments are controlled by big corporations, television and other media, banks, schools, religions – all pulling in separate directions – disease is the almost inevitable natural result.

There is also the factor to consider that group consciousness dictates that people will become sick in certain circumstances or situations. The mind believes in the illness, and the body responds by "catching" the illness. This is another example of the Universe bending to match the commanded frequency of the individual or group. The Universe is a perfect living machine, and it always responds "Yes!" This is why 3D/low energy can be considered a blessing; there is a time delay between the wish and its fulfillment. This is a good thing when a human is first practicing his manifestation skills! Otherwise, each time a child wished his brother would "shut up and die," he might. So you see, Beloved, this is really a safety mechanism.

Go and think on this some more, and we will speak again tomorrow.

MAY 30, 2016
AM, HOME

Archangel Michael:

Thank you for speaking with us this morning, Beloved. It was wonderful to tell you through your pendulum that your DNA has eight strands connected and has converted over 95% to the new crystalline matrix. You will notice many changes, Beloved. This is what you've been waiting for!

You would have already noticed some of the smaller, subtler, more fundamental changes, but your human senses are not yet operating at full capacity. Someone who had not seen you in several months would definitely see many changes. This is the gift of perspective, and it is indeed a gift, because it reinforces the idea that you are all connected and shall rely on each other to live the fullest version of your lives.

Your team from Egypt is here, Beloved, and they wish to speak to you. The "spokesperson" for this collective group/hive called "Asyriath" asks that you refer to him as Jareth (he is a gender neutral being but has pulled the masculine aspect out of your mind and has asked to be assigned male attributes during this conversation). Jareth, welcome.

Jareth:

Indeed it is a pleasure to communicate with you today. You are part of our Soul-level consciousness and we have incarnated together many times in Egypt. We know each other very well, and it gives me great joy to speak to you again, my old friend! Thank you for acknowledging us, for we Asyriaths have a long, rich and beautiful history on your planet Earth. Our galaxy is far away; but, like many others, we sent a delegation to earth to assist with the Ascension. Of course we knew of your participation "behind the Iron Curtain" (laughter), and we are most pleased that you are again Awake enough to know us! We know all emotions very well, because as a collective species we feel them all, from everyone, all the time. It is a rich tapestry of different colors and textures which fluctuates constantly. It is beautiful on our planet – the triple Suns cause much heat, so we have many tropical plants and animals; and although we do not "eat," we do see from your memory archives that our system would be considered to have a long growing season! We also have much water, although not nearly as much as Earth does.

We are here to assist you by accessing long-buried memories of Egypt and its amazing technologies which have been long forgotten. We are master builders and architects, and in your "past" (how strange to use linear words to describe Time, which everyone knows is infinite!) the Egyptians, and later the Romans, used much of our wisdom to build great structures and gardens using our technology and planning. We hope to awaken enough souls to make this technology accessible again to you.

We shall give you some examples. The huge pyramids now standing on the Giza plateau were built using our technology. Master builders from our planet found that the instantaneous manifestation so common on other worlds could not exist in the dense energy of 3D Earth, so they went to Plan B: employ some of the technologies played with by the children of our planet. One such technology – really no more than a toy – is levitation. We taught humans of that era how to focus their energies on the center point of the mass of an object, and how to command it to move. Essentially, the blocks of the pyramids soared through the air and neatly stacked themselves. Some had to be moved slightly in the beginning, because, like children, the blocks were not set down in perfect alignment. But soon, the builders could set a stone perfectly on the first try. The great pyramid of Giza took 12 of your Earth years to build, not because slave workers had to haul blocks up an artificial ramp, but rather because of the sheer number of blocks in that structure.

Another technology, a simple cutting tool guided by the mind, allowed us to cut each block perfectly, with equal edges and no waste. The blocks were then levitated out and moved over to be placed.

A third technology, a liquid that can change one substance into another (again, a child's toy), was used to "decorate" the various elements. There was once a lovely flat covering on the Great Pyramid, much like a skin, made of pure gold to reflect the sun and channel the heat into the center of the pyramid via a large *heliakyte* crystal (like a large diamond) at the apex of the pyramid. A heliakyte can harness and focus any energy in any direction, depending on how the stone is shaped. Your classic round diamond with many facets on top and a single point at the bottom is the perfect shape for such a task: the many facets collect energies from all angles and focus them down into a single point. This energy flowed through the exact center of the pyramid, through a small chamber in which a high priestess lay. She modulated the energy and sent it downward into the earth, producing a standing energy wave which could be harnessed to power lights, run a grain mill, or any of a thousand other uses.

Archangel Michael:

We feel your energy flagging, Beloved. Go and eat, and We will speak again.

(LATER THAT DAY)

Jareth:

We spoke earlier of the technologies used in Earth's past to build and create huge structures such as the pyramids, the Colosseum, and the aqueduct – and we spoke of three specific children's toys that were modified to be used in 3D: levitation, a cutting tool and a liquid form changer. These were used because the density of the 3D time/space did not allow for the usual instant manifestation with just two people creating anything (one to hold the inner form and one to encase it in walls, sides, etc.). The fourth and final piece of the puzzle is a kind of dust made from heliakyte crystals – this powers the building and is the "go juice" that allows things to occur. The dust is something like electricity: without it, a television is just a simple metal box; with it, you can watch 1,000 channels or surf the internet. Now you will ask why stone construction needs the equivalent of electricity, and we will tell you! The H-dust (this is the common name for the substance) is not just a power source, it almost creates a living object. The pyramid used a giant heliakyte crystal to focus energy to power machines to clean the air and water, grow plants, control magnetic fields and more and H-dust has similar properties. With it, the aqueduct transports clean water through tunnels that remain constantly in perfect repair and the pyramid provides energy for a large city.

So, what happened to these systems? When the time cycle came around to the top and began to dip downward again – as part of the procession of the equinoxes – the knowledge of these technologies was gradually lost and was replaced with fully "manual" versions of those activities. It became necessary to *repair* things, and *rebuild* things, and the effortless systems were forgotten. Only recently have these systems come back, although none are yet back to full use. But soon!

Thank you once again, friend, for hearing our wisdom. We are here helping more than you know, and in the future we have more to tell you. Goodbye for now.

MAY 31, 2016
PM, HOME

Archangel Michael:

We have much to tell you tonight, but we hear the many questions in your mind. Please proceed and We shall answer.

Michele: When Will my DNA be fully crystalline?

AAM: As with all time-based questions, beloved, it is impossible to say for sure. The probabilities indicate that the changeover will be completed by the end of this week. You are currently at 96% and the final stages have begun.

Michele: When will I notice changes in my physical body and mental state?

AAM: Beloved, there are already so many changes that you do not see! If you were not so close to the process, you would already notice the many changes.

Michele: When can I start commanding changes and seeing instant results (instant manifestation)?

Archangel Michael: Now, beloved one! The changes will appear within a few days; there is still a time delay because of the dense nature of Earth's energy field, but in short, *now!*

Michele: When will I be able to bilocate?

Archangel Michael: Again, We have no definite date, but your system is clearing debris at an unprecedented rate. If you could see from Our vantage point, you would be so assured and so very heartened. All We can answer to this question is "very, very soon."

Michele: When will the publishers show up for the books?

Archangel Michael: When you are done typing them! (laughter) In this case, Beloved, you yourself are the delay. We encourage you to use the next few weeks while away from

Michele D. Baker

home to finish transcribing the other notebook – then the next step will appear. As We know you so well, We choose not to allow you to pre-know this information as you would focus on *it* rather than on finishing the task at hand. We help you most successfully by encouraging you to finish tasks in order. In other words, get moving: the sooner the better to get the writing career off the ground!

Michele: Is my Twin Flame nearby?

Archangel Michael: Yes, and he is ready to meet you, too; and no, it's not Dwayne Johnson. (laughter) [Author's note: I dreamed last night that I met my ideal match, but somehow I had forgotten I was already married to Dwayne "The Rock" Johnson.] Your Twin Flame is a very nice man, and in no way resembles a wrestler. (more laughter) We will tell you no more, except that he does have blue eyes. We will speak again tomorrow.

JUNE 1, 2016
AM, HOME

Archangel Michael:

Welcome to a new day, Beloved. Today is a remarkable day, a "7" day – the first of June (6 + 1 numerologically), sevens are connected to romantic relationships (indeed, relationships of all kinds). It is also a new trecena in the Mayan calendar,[3] one of mirror/reflection and inner work. You have so little left to do, and yet so much lies yet ahead of you. We are so happy that the part of your journey that you've long awaited is finally at hand!

Yes, beloved the mirror was correct. You have lost weight, and your skin is clearer; this was not a trick your mind was playing on you. We told you yesterday that the cellular recombination was nearly complete, and so it is the new structure is much more responsive, as you will see. You can change it at will. Your diet, and your preferred foods have already changed, have they not? You gave up sweets with nary a look backward. We feel your disbelief that it could ever be so easy, but really, Beloved, these are simple matters. The real fun is soon to come: bilocation for you is "just around the corner." Yes, you will be able to take objects with you, and yes, some living creatures, too. Not all humans can go; it depends on their frequency, and some are not yet ready to "jump." You will know who can go.

Type on the book a bit more today, Beloved. We are ready to guide your next steps.

---

[3] The Mayan calendar is an ancient alternative to the more-common Gregorian calendar. See Appendix D.

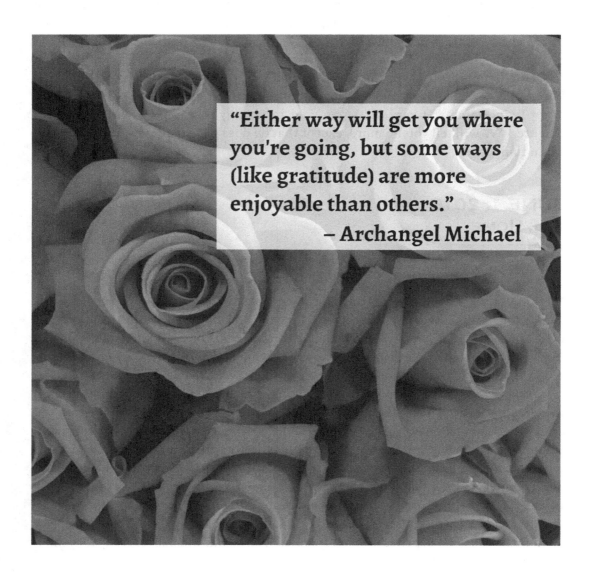

"Either way will get you where you're going, but some ways (like gratitude) are more enjoyable than others."
– Archangel Michael

Michele D. Baker

JUNE 2, 2016
AM, HOME

Archangel Michael:

Yes, Beloved, you got Our messages perfectly this morning – your new DNA is coming online and among other things, your five senses have been heightened. Your hearing, which was always quite good, has improved significantly. Your sight, too – you will notice that you can read close things again. Your sense of smell was always acute, although you had trained it not to smell dirty cat litter (laughter), and you will notice your skin is hypersensitive to temperature, wind and ambient moisture. Many of these senses will seem very normal, as you were already using them at near-peak capacity. But now they will seem "supercharged."

The physical changes you ordered have already begun as well: you are correct when you wondered if your stomach was flatter. Yes, it is! The changes in your DNA, combined with your cessation of eating sugar, have worked quickly; although you don't see it that way, We assure you that this is quite a fast transition! If you had not done so much foundational prework, the process would have been quite different. This is also because of "disease" (dis-ease) in this time, Beloved, as people experience symptoms and changes, they can't explain, and think there is something wrong. There is nothing wrong – in fact, there is *something very right* happening to most humans: they are ascending quickly. Your task, Beloved, is to do it as a member of the vanguard, to "blaze a trail" and show your fellow humans what is possible. In this, we assure you, you are on the far left of the curve! [Author's Note: I've been reading Simon Sinek's "Find Your Why" which references people being "early adopters" of some ideas, while waiting until the end before accepting other ideas.]

Today you must type, Beloved – the optimal time to send the book to publish approaches/increases in potential. Now go and have a wonderful day!

JUNE 3, 2016
PM, HOME

Archangel Michael:

No, Beloved... Sam Heughan [of the "Outlander" TV series] is not for you. While he is a lovely actor, and by human standards quite good-looking (laughter), he is on an entirely

Michele D. Baker

different life path. What do you feel from him is the openness of a pure soul – nothing romantic. We feel your distress at the emotional rollercoaster you've been on the last few days, and we can assure you that it's almost over. Your newly upgraded systems are "coming online" and they are still calibrating, a process which throws the switches from full off to full on and back again trying to learn your preferred levels. This is also what was happening with your hearing in the night… but it's better now, yes? And your short vision is back, yes? And yes, you are losing weight as your new DNA brings your body back into alignment. These are truly miraculous times, Beloved. You must take a moment and enjoy them, for *this is what you've been waiting for*! We rejoice with you as you take these first steps into a completely new way of being.

We are so proud of the job you are doing, writing daily. Now We wish to reprioritize the book – it is time to prepare your next steps, which means you need a typed version. Finish up, beloved the next world of travel and fun awaits!

JUNE 5, 2016
PM, HOME

Archangel Michael:

We come to you with great gladness, Beloved, the time is here for you and our messages to enter the world. Please finish the transcribing: that will trigger the publisher to find you.

More and more you see and notice red-haired men: this is due to a lifetime you had among those peoples – the beings of Andromeda with red hair, fair skin and green eyes. They are beings of great integrity whose contributions to galactic civilization are vast. They are also known for their impartial decision-making and well-known as lawmakers and arbiters because of their great wisdom. They attract you because, like many humans, you have a strand of genetic material from this race. You also have Reptilian DNA, which gives you clarity of vision and the ability to focus on the task at hand. From your Sirian ancestors, you get your highly logical mind and aptitude for science and mathematics. Your language and creative sides, especially your writing skills, come from the planet that orbits the star and constellation Maya; this planet is also called Maya (or Maja). The Asyriaths are of the Sirian group of people, and those brave communicators and adventurers are also in your DNA – these are the very qualities that served them well in ancient Egypt.

These are the main bloodline strands in your physical DNA, now coming online and manifesting because of the completion of the DNA reconfiguration that occurred in the last 48 hours. Congratulations are in order, Beloved, for you are now an entirely different species of being than other humans! This is the birthright, and the soon-coming goal of all beings now incarnate in 4D/5D Earth. Within 50 years your world will look nothing like it does now – it will be a veritable paradise. Such is the coming news: that all creatures will ascend in their physical bodies – just as you have – and this process will awaken the collective consciousness in all humans, and no longer only a few selected Ascended Masters. Get the messages out: show people what it looks like to live in the New, and in the Now. This is your destiny and your mission. We are so happy for you!

All things continue to move very fast: delight in the new of each day and the interesting things that will occur. Expect daily miracles – and you will get them!

With love, We remain, The Ascended Beings of the Galactic Light and Your Team

JUNE 7, 2016
AM, BILOXI, MISSISSIPPI

Archangel Michael:

Beloved Daughter of Light: your purpose here on the coast is simply to hold the space and allow participants to enjoy their experiences here. We have seen that you are doing a good job of this, everything is going well, and your people are allowing themselves to exhale. All is well.

JUNE 10, 2016
PM, GULFPORT, MISSISSIPPI

Archangel Michael:

We have missed speaking with you, too, Beloved One! As you do, We feel the pain of separation, the pangs of conscience that you haven't written this whole week, but We do not assign negative connotations to those feelings. They simply *are*. The sweetness of our reunion (although of course we were never really apart!) is pleasant also for Us.

We wish to update you on your new biological organism and give you a few pointers on how to control the vehicle you now inhabit: for your body has become an intergalactic vessel capable of moving you between dimensions, and thus between physical "spaces." (This supposes there is something "other" or "separate" from the endless Now – which there is not – but it is a convenient way to explain to someone who still primarily sees situations through a 3D, language-based context.) Your newly upgraded vehicle will move to a new location at your command, so now you must learn the new commands! Much like when you learned to drive a stick shift car, at first it was unfamiliar and difficult, but soon became completely second nature and an *easy* task, even a *fun* task. So it is with bilocation.

First, envision the new location: feel the breeze, taste the flavor, smell the scents and imagine yourself there. Then, take a small step "up" into the 4D lower harmonics, and you will almost be in a slipstream – you will be able to see the Earth moving below you. Next, "walk" to your desired destination, and then take a small step "down" again to the new place. You'll get the hang of it soon enough! Since time (little "t") moves at a much faster rate in the slipstream, you will move instantly from A to B in Earth time. You will appear to have simply vanished, then rematerialized in the new place. Travel to anywhere on Earth can be achieved in this way. You will easily see where you are going: no rematerializing inside a wall or in a river!

This process is also used for travel to other places in your Galaxy that can sustain an oxygen-breathing vessel, or to other dimensions, according to your level of spiritual access and ability.

Travel *without* taking the body is actually much easier, but the point of ascending in the body is to take your memories with you. Of course, the process works in reverse, and as "home" is the most well-known frequency for you, "popping back home" will be as easy as breathing. We will help you learn this skill, Beloved – your DNA now supports such transportation ability. We are mainly in pure energy form here, and so your movement of an actual solid body is a novelty even for Us. We look forward with great expectations to seeing you "make this leap" very soon. We sense your questions, and We will answer.

Yes, Beloved, you can take some objects with you – such as clothing or a piece of luggage – and even some people may travel with you, too. You must be careful, though, as they can slow down or stop the process if their minds are not clear, or if they suddenly tune into "Paris" while you're trying to go to Rome. But frequency is the key here, so if both parties are concentrating on "Rome," there should be little problem. In short, beloved, you are now free to roam your earth and your Galaxy at will. Your longtime dream – which We implanted! – to have breakfast in Cairo, is now possible!

JUNE 11, 2016
PM, GULFPORT, MISSISSIPPI

Archangel Michael:

Beloved, the voice you heard in the shower this morning was the "default" voice of your new body machine! And yes, you did turn on/initiate several dozen "programs" this morning, including the languages program; the super healing program; the bilocation and other transportation programs; the healthy body programs; the music, piano and singing programs; writing and photography; and more. Funny – you did *not* turn on or enable the romantic partner/love or money programs. In other words, you are currently focused internally, so this will "come online" later. And yes, that was quite a lot of downloads to process, so 48 hours is a good estimate before you can expect to see real changes.

We are so glad to see you happily exploring the new "features" much like you would a new camera or a new car. Although your newly upgraded vehicle is both – and more than both! – you also activated the Akashic Records function, which means you now have access to the archives, and can recall, review, or replay any event you wish by simply looking in the Records.

Have We also mentioned how proud We are of your quick adaptation to this new system? These changes normally occur over many millennia, or even tens or hundreds of thousands of years. But your species is poised on the brink of an accelerated leap into galactic brotherhood, and membership in that "organization" requires some substantial growth/acceleration on the part of humankind. This is your greatest potential and your Divine birthright from the beginning, and here you are, as a species, taking your first steps into the New. No longer are you *Homo sapiens sapiens,* Beloved, but rather *Homo galacticus*!

We love you, so get some rest.

JUNE 16, 2016
AM, ODESSA, TEXAS

Archangel Michael:

We have missed you, Beloved! There is much to tell you, but we will save most for tonight – it is imperative you write this evening!

Michele D. Baker

Gratitude Game #4

INNOVATION IMAGINATION

I use this game whenever I'm feeling sad or sorry for myself.
It's also known as "I'm so happy now that I..."

Get ready - Walk on the beach, relax in the tub, or sit under a tree.
Whatever makes you happy! Play **Game #1: "Ground/Center/
Shield"** and then begin innovating. Here's an example from a friend
who wanted a new job:

*"I'm so happy now that I've got a new job researching sunken wrecks.
I'm working 30 hours a week and get 6 weeks of paid vacation.
My new salary is double! Company car, vision and dental, too. This
new job is great. Thanks, Universe!"*

Now you try... put all the details in there. Weight loss. New car.
New partner. More money. Shoot for the moon. (Even if you fail,
you'll land among the stars.)

P.S. My friend got a new job with more money, less hours, and
"wreck diving" as part of his job description. (True story.)

Michele D. Baker

The encounter last night with the hotel clerk was an example of the old way (blame orientation) and the new way (cooperation orientation) coming in contact. The young woman has long lived in a world where blame is the norm, and she has great fear of being wrong or making a mistake. Feel compassion for her, Beloved: she is asleep still, but is beginning to wake up, and is very confused.

As for the storm, you and your mother called it to you! There was an expectation on your part to see a thunderstorm, and so one appeared. The intensity matched the intensity of your desire to see one. This was an example of your manifestation abilities now, Beloved – so use your powers with great care and with great consideration.

Today will be a lovely day – the caverns will refresh you, so go out and enjoy them and come back to us tonight. Be well!

LATER THAT DAY
PM, ROSWELL, NEW MEXICO

Archangel Michael:

Yes, Beloved, We see you practicing your unending compassion and it is pleasing to Us! We watch with great joy as you spread a light wherever you go. Carlsbad Caverns were wonderful to you because they felt like your home planet. Sirius is a hot planet with a climate much like Egypt, but there are many cold spots and lots of clear green water, which has a thick consistency like syrup. It is very pleasant to be in this water, which is perfect for the body. Yes, the beings on that planet are also incarnate, and look similar to humans, but with a more feline appearance. While the movie Avatar was not quite right, the native/indigenous Sirians look much like the Pandorans from that movie: taller than humans and with faintly leonine features. Their skin tones range from blue to green to golden, with golden being the most common. There is no distinction among the Sirians with regard to skin color – it is a matter of individual preference and as they have control of their physical bodies, they can change skin colors at will, often to suit their moods.

These people are masters of genetic engineering and have created many species to populate the planets in your galaxy. Each species is formed from donor material from the host world, and then mixed and engineered to suit the needs and specifications of that world. Many species were created this way, and each is fully gifted with 100% genetic autonomy – the Sirian geneticists do not create slave races! The human prototype was changed once it was placed on Earth, remember – the

Sirian creators of the original form never intended it to be changed or altered in such a fashion.

Sirius is a lush planet filled with many brilliant species of plants and animals. The Sirians do not consume any of the species there: they exist on a manufactured "foodstuff" that is nutritious and contains exactly the necessary ingredients to maintain the physical form. The Sirians do not eat the other animals or plants because their bodies do not process food as human bodies do, and also because they would not wish to harm any other being or creature – they live in a symbiotic circle with every "rock," "tree," "bird," and "fish" on Sirius.

Like humans, Sirians breathe a gaseous mixture/atmosphere, but their planet contains much more nitrogen and carbon dioxide, and very little oxygen – and their atmosphere also contains sulfur; that mineral assures that every "skin" on Sirius has a beautiful glow!

Thank you for speaking with Us tonight, Beloved. Sleep well!

JUNE 17, 2016
PM, Santa Fe, New Mexico

Archangel Michael:

Greetings this evening, Beloved! We feel your much-earned weariness, so We will not keep you long. But, We do wish to address why you love this part of your Earth so much!

Your main home planet, Sirius, looks a lot like New Mexico and Arizona. There are large mountain ranges and what on Earth would be considered high desert. It can be hot, but there is much water on Sirius and its consistency (remember, like syrup) causes it to stay in one place more easily than Earth water. The climate is cooler during some times of the year, and Sirius also has what could be termed "seasons:" a rainy and cool season and a hotter, drier season. This is also geographic – you came from the cool, wet part but always loved the hot, dry part! We could tell you much more, but We feel your attention flagging. We love you, and goodnight.

JUNE 19, 2016
PM, TAOS, NEW MEXICO

Archangel Michael:

Greetings, Beloved, from all Souls in your Team and in the celestial realms. We thank you for your service to Us and to Mother Gaia. This evening, Archangel Gabriel wishes to speak to you.

Archangel Gabriel:

Most beautiful evening to you, Dear One, close to Our hearts and special to all! I come to you this evening with a message from your grandparents who are with us in the spirit realm – they wish you to know that they are helping you write and publish the magnificent treatise that is the first book, and they wish to impart all blessings and love to you on this heavenly journey. Your grandfathers are with you – all three of them – and they are watching wholeheartedly as you perform your writing tasks so admirably. They are close to you on this celebration of Father's Day in the United States and they are also helping bring you and your Twin Flame together. There is great love there for you and these men love you very much; they are assisting from the celestial realms!

Archangel Michael:

Thank you, Gabriel. You must continue with your mission, Beloved. All is in Divine Right Time, but We also believe "the sooner, the better." (laughter) Good night!

JUNE 21, 2016
PM, FAYETTEVILLE, ARKANSAS

Archangel Michael:

Hello and greetings, Beloved! We feel your physical and mental exhaustion and We wish to explain why this is so. Your body – although it is entirely crystalline-based DNA now and with all strands connected – is still in a state of change over to the new configuration. Remember, this is a process that normally takes eons, and you are doing it in weeks and months. We laugh to ourselves at this statement, because (of course) time does not exist! But, as we have explained before, Time (capital T) does exist, and each event or occurrence does have its own unique Divine Right Timing (remember the previous example of a human baby requiring nine months to gestate). Thus, you are still caught between the old and the New, although We assure you that you are much closer to the New end than the old! Think of this changeover as a complex computer requiring time to boot up; indeed, the amazing "machine" that is your physical vehicle is very much like a computer. Your energy will stabilize soon, We promise.

We have planned a special surprise for you in Eureka Springs tomorrow: watch for it. We will be sure and "poke you" so you recognize it when you see it! Good night for now.

JULY 1, 2016
PM, HOME

Archangel Michael:

Hello, Dearest One – We have missed speaking to you and have impulsed you often these last days to write and to transcribe. You have exercised your free will to sleep and read, and We honor such, while asking again that you work on your book!

Every wonderful thing awaits you in due course, Beloved, and your finishing of the book is the key that unlocks all the rest. It is literally a gateway to the next steps, and you must be brave enough to take them.

There are so many out there whom you could help with this information – We urge you to stop procrastinating and step into your power, for this is your birthright, your destiny, and the promise you made when you came to earth this time. We understand your hesitation and even your fear of the unknown before you, coupled perhaps with a shade of disbelief at the time actually being at hand/being the Now. After being told for so long that the "promised land" is just beyond the next corner, it can be difficult to accept when the final corner actually is turned! We know this, and We and all others are watching over you in every moment ("every-now"). There is nothing to fear – you literally cannot make a mistake! But you must begin again; the Now is here. This is your sacred promise – We love you so much and will guide your every step. Goodnight.

Michele D. Baker

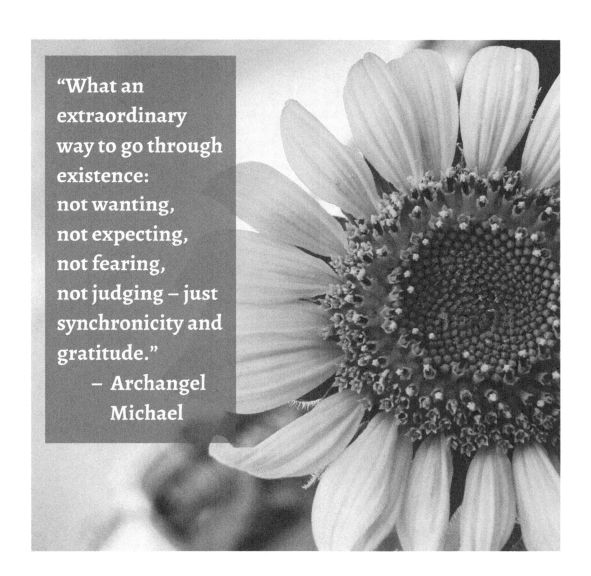

"What an extraordinary way to go through existence:
not wanting,
not expecting,
not fearing,
not judging – just synchronicity and gratitude."
– Archangel Michael

Michele D. Baker

Archangel Michael:

Welcome back to Us, Beloved! We are happy you "had a talk with yourself" last night and were able to moderate your anger. We feel your frustration at many events in your world: shootings of unarmed people and police officers; destruction of art and literature; the disregard and unfairness with which humans treat each other and the planet; and much more. It is good that you *feel*, Beloved. Even those feelings you deem "bad" or "sad" are so important, and you are learning not to judge. This is a mighty lesson that humans have struggled with since "the fall" to two strands of DNA.

We also hear some guilt, some regret, at not yet being done with the transcriptions. Here, We say to you, "do not be afraid!" All is in perfect balance, and when your free will aligns you to your mission, nothing can stop you. We say to you, We are proud of you and We cherish you and your service to humanity. Let all be as it should be – there is no way to stop the Ascension – only to slow it down.

There is much to be grateful for here, Beloved – this is what you've been waiting for! All is here in this Now. The life you were born to lead is at hand: no longer is it at some unspecified "future" moment. This is the new Now! My beloved brother, the Archangel Gabriel, wishes to speak.

Archangel Gabriel:

Greetings to you, Exalted Sister and Beloved One! Your service to this planet and to your fellow humans is a divine blessing and you are to be thanked. We here in the Celestial Realms know what it is to co-create and to allow to spring forth great and wondrous miracles for the benefit of this Universe and the God-source. Thus it is that We come to you with great joy to assist in the miracle that is your unique contribution to the human experience in this Now. The limpid pools of imagination are tapped, bringing forth these words into reality and onto the page. Thus are the heavens united with the Earthly plane and thus is the message revealed. Your word structures and Our insight and perspectives combine into a document of power, beauty and hope for all.

Never before has it been possible to ascend to the next plane while in the context of an incarnate body. Thus, We share the marvelous news of a new era, a new Age, the dawn of a time that will see humankind unveil his memory and step into the fully actualized human he once was, and is now again.

Thank you, Beloved, for allowing Us to speak through you, for allowing Us to co-create with you this marvelous book! We shall provide the inspiration, and you shall provide the pen. Thus will our lesson be shared. Thank you!

JULY 11, 2016
PM, HOME

Archangel Michael:

Greetings, Beloved, on this beautiful summer evening. We know you are on your way to a meeting, and We wish to speak with you briefly on your health.

Your upgrade is complete, as We have told you before: you are now a fully ascended and awake Homo galacticus being and no longer Homo sapiens. You did have questions on why it's taking so long to manifest the changes, and We refer you both to this message and to the passage you sent Our Wayne about Time/time (capital T versus small T) from "All We Need Is Love: In Service to the Light Book One:"

Archangel Michael:

The end of time is at hand, and the end of all things that do not serve you or serve Love. *This is good news!* We wish to speak to you now of the difference between time (small "t") and Time (capital "T"). Time (small "t"), an artificial construct, has kept humans stuck, mired in a system that prevents and stifles their creativity, their ability to co-create. The nature of time is that you perceive a *lack* of it. There have been phrases, too, to further reinforce this belief and inhibit your Power: "time is money," "there's never enough time," "what time is it?" Then add a system of calendars to enforce further an erroneous idea of time. In truth, time does not exist – it is simply the way your five senses perceive it. Time does not "pass," but rather there is an Endless Now that stretches out forward and backward, up and down, indeed, in all directions like a sphere.

You, Vessel, know this from Sacred Geometry. Begin with a point or a dot (the Divine Feminine aspect), then extend the dot into a line (the Divine Masculine aspect) – this is the first movement. Then the point extends in all directions simultaneously; a sphere emerges (Totality). This sphere represents one moment in "time" but also an entire universe: "as above, so below." One point on the surface of the sphere extends to a second point, and the process continues – a vesica piscis is formed. One sphere becomes two, two become four, four become eight. It is not so much that the spheres *divide* as that they *birth* each other. Thus is all matter created, from the tiniest atom to an entire planet.

One important thing to understand: "time" as you perceive it is really made up of a series of moments (Nows), each one a sphere, a Universe in itself. These spheres, these moments, these Nows... all string together to create what humans perceive as linear "time." But remember, each sphere is infinite in all directions; thus, is real Time (capital "T") continuous in all directions, and not linear at all, except in your memory, which is selectively choosing moments to remember.

Your human brain could remember all the moments if you wished it to, but here we bump against a second limitation imposed by the 3D construct: judgment. Some memories are discarded as having less value, or as being bad, good, happy, sad, etc., and so they are categorized in the mind. Every moment, every Now, is sacred and precious, and is both "over in an instant" and infinite, simultaneously! What a beautiful thing to realize: that every moment is a gift (yes, We hear the cliché in your mind: "that's why it's called the 'present'!"), and an infinity in and of itself.

This lesson, of time and Time and the nature of the Universe, is a key concept to understand. Each thing happens in its own perfect Time and as such, Time does exist as a construct, but only as a tool of Creation. For example, Time passes between the fertilization of an egg and the birth of a new human. There is a process that must occur before the human can be born. Thus, Time is necessary for progress, but not for process. We will try to explain further, as We feel your confusion here, Beloved.

Time (small "t") does not exist, but Time (capital "T") is necessary for the progress of the processes, or for the process to progress. In other words, time (as defined by a clock or a calendar) does not exist and is an artificial construct. Nine months on a calendar do not exist, but it takes a human baby nine months to mature for birth. The passage of time is but a blink of any eye to Us, and because time is malleable it is flexible. To paraphrase dialogue from a movie you recently saw (We cannot now access which movie, Beloved, our apologies!): "An hour spent with your Beloved seems like a minute, but a minute with your hand on a hot pan handle seems like an hour." Do you not see how time (small "t") is subjective, accidental, and ultimately malleable? There is a better way to explain this – We will search your memory archives and find it and we will speak again.

(pause)

Time (capital "T") is circular and fractal. Imagine a marble rolling around the outside of a beach ball. Eventually, it will roll back around to your "side." Time is the beach ball, a microcosm of the Universal macrocosm. You, Beloved, are the marble.

Once again, [your cat] Geoffrey – who is a subset, or a splinter, or a microcosm of your Angelic Guide Geoffrey – is helping you. You can *feel* the love this being has for you – every fiber of his body longs to help you. [Your other cats] Mica and Lillie are helping, too, by modulating and moderating your sleeping times. They buffer the downloads and monitor transmissions (dreams) from Higher Realms, enabling you to sleep better. Yes, Beloved One, your sleep would be much less, and much less restful, without their assistance. This is why Lillie sits at your feet and Mica insists on sleeping on or near your head. They "tune" the transmissions to allow for ease of assimilation.

Back to the topic of Time – generous portions of Time/time are allotted to your "upgrades" and "downloads," to use terms you are now familiar with. We send information to you in a waking state (these Messages/Transmissions) and in your sleep (lessons, DNA shifts, prophetic dreams, healing energy). Many, many star beings are assisting with this evening work, including a Sirian female whose appearance is that of a dark brown Lion. It is no accident, nor is it a coincidence, that you were born in August under a Leo sun and also the Leo moon! Your Cat nature is one of the gifts we gave you, to allow Messages from these leonine/feline beings to permeate your conscious world. For cat energy is the energy of rest and of pure potential. Cats can move from sleeping to springing in a very short time. They are efficient at conserving energy until it is needed, and then releasing it at 100 percent. (Yes, Beloved, this brings to mind a scene from *Star Wars: The Phantom Menace* in which Qui Gon Jin is using this resting technique between fights with Darth Maul in the energy barrier corridor.)

Cats are also Masters of Time because they always live in the Now, in this moment.

OK, Beloved, We have found an image for you of Time that may help when you share it with others: think of a pearl necklace. Each bead is a sphere, a Now, a Moment and they all touch on the string. Now, We know what you will say! A pearl necklace is a linear construct! No, Beloved – it is a closed loop, circling over and over, and because pearls are organic, they are unique, never seen the same way twice. We offer another image of Time: that of a river flowing. There is an Earth saying: "You can never swim in the same river twice." Because in every moment, every time you swim again, there is a new Now. And yes, a river is also circular – going to the sea, to be carried up as rain and deposited back into the mountains where it begins again.

Why is this discussion of time and Time relevant or necessary? Because Time is real, whereas time is not. In short, time is an accident of the way your nervous system processes stimuli and the information from the five senses. Calendars, deadlines, due dates, age, start and end times... all these are illusory, joint illusions by the group, who have decided that when the little hands on the clock both point up, we all agree to call this "noon" and it will correspond with the sun at its highest point in the sky.

But too strong a belief in this artificial construct, when the illusion becomes a shared acceptance of reality, then do the problems begin. Then, shortages, deficiencies, and lack can occur. "I'll only live eighty years." "The meeting begins at noon, so don't be late." "I didn't have enough time to finish that project." All these and thousands more examples! Conflict arises because Time and time are confused in the minds of many.

This folds into a larger discussion of abundance, Beloved. For now, go and get ready. You have somewhere to be at four o'clock! (laughter)

Archangel Michael continues:

The changes have taken effect, Beloved One, and if you had the benefit of distance, these would be very evident. You are living inside the changes, so you are not as easily able to see them. But We assure you, you are a much different being than you were even three or six months ago. You have lost weight, your eyesight and hearing have improved, your skin tone and elasticity have begun to "regress," and you are reverting – although it feels slowly – to the body of a 35 year old: strong and vibrant, yet mature in all ways. We also noted your request to cease your monthly cycle but to keep the hormonal balance of younger female. We have also put this request "into the queue" and it shall be granted soon your changes are complete. You can begin playing around with the instantaneous co-creation feature, which We know you will enjoy! We laughed earlier at your facial changes while you were waiting. Yes, Beloved, all these improvements will be available and more! And yes, they will be instantaneous. Now, enjoy your food, for this kind of heavy eating has a limit, too. (Laughter)

JULY 21, 2016
PM, HOME

Archangel Michael:

Hello, Beloved – We are so happy to feel your energy in the pen again! Your work on the book is coming along nicely, and we wish to reiterate that you are on time and on task. The book will be finished and published very soon now – the potentials have coalesced into a beautiful crystalline form with the book at the center, radiating light outward from its central point. Soon, we shall impulse you to lay out a preliminary design for the cover, and We shall choose the size at last. All things in their Divine Right Timing!

Gratitude Game #5

LOVE THYSELF

Every morning as you brush your teeth and comb your hair, really look at yourself in the mirror. Speaking out loud, point out your best features to yourself. Admire those things you love best about your appearance:

"You have got the most gorgeous brown eyes, my dear!"

Then move along to the features you don't love best, and praise them anyway, as if it's already true:

"That flat tummy sure is sexy, you absolute fox!"

Finally, give yourself a huge hug, blow yourself a kiss, and say:

"I LOVE YOU, YOU AMAZING CREATURE!"

(Bonus points for doing the same for your spouse, kids, coworkers, friends, neighbors...)

Michele D. Baker

Your talk with Our Marcie today was apt: you were correct to tell her that she has nothing to do with this situation. She is the catalyst, the activating agent, for a lesson for others, among them former colleagues. We do not wish to say this was karmic, but there was a lesson there which had not yet been assimilated and learned and this is another attempt at allowing all parties to get the lesson. Marcie was simply the convenient excuse, as you were in the past with others. Your counsel to her to remain detached was a helpful piece of confirmation for her and she should allow events to unfold unhindered.

We are pleased also to tell you, Beloved, that your supposition was indeed correct: finishing this book will indeed finish the lesson of finding a way around the roadblocks. We feel your guilt over past instances where you have excitedly begun a project or an enterprise and then, hitting this roadblock, have put them away. *There is no reason for guilt or disappointment!* This was all a test, a lesson you set for yourself to break down this very barrier. You have done it before, and you will complete this lesson upon publishing the book. Your internal war will be won and be over. We heartily congratulate you!

On another topic, the potentials strongly indicate that your friend's father will pass over to this Realm very soon. He is tired and weak in his body, and his spirit is too strong to be contained much longer. What a relief that he will finally be released from this struggle. His family will of course mourn his loss, but they, too, are weary of struggling to help him, and he can merely subsist. Many powerful beings are crossing over at this time, brave souls whose talents are needed to balance the final remnants of the Dark, which is fighting tooth and nail to keep its tenuous grip on your world. But the Light always wins, Beloved – for even darkness still falls somewhere on the spectrum of light!

Finally, We wish to tell you that another great event is just up on the horizon – your Twin Flame approaches. Again, the publishing of the book is the catalyst: truly, this event will mark a milestone in the path of your eventful and gracious life. This Beloved Soul will connect with you as part of the book process. We will give you no more details, except to say he is coming!

JULY 23, 2016
PM, COLUMBUS, MISSISSIPPI

Archangel Michael:

We feel the pain all around you, Beloved, and We grieve with the family so much. This precious soul is fighting to leave, and he will do so, despite the heroic efforts of the competent doctors around him. He was indeed crying out to you to leave, Beloved – his Soul trapped in a fleshly body that has stopped responding to his conscious commands. This was all pre-contracted – the illness, the early death of the flesh – by all parties, although they do not remember it. These lessons are here to put people into their emotional bodies – *to really feel* – and the circumstances are allowing them to learn their lessons well.

Thus will these Beloved Souls learn a new configuration of "family," and thus will they have the opportunity to learn that love is not confined to incarnate bodies. When people love each other truly, they can never be separated: in truth, there is always togetherness and never separation, except in the dualistic illusion of 3D.

You are doing well there, Beloved, helping with the routine to ensure comfort for all in the house. Do not underestimate the importance of these seemingly insignificant tasks! The family needs to have food prepared and laundry done. The dog is doing his part as a member of the family! You are ensuring that the family stays running, and you are always invaluable to Renee. We love and honor your service to this family, Beloved. Come to us again tomorrow.

JULY 28, 2016
PM, PETERSHAM, MASSACHUSETTS

Archangel Michael:

Such is your life, Beloved: here one moment, there the next! Your longed-for transportation system of bilocation is close at hand and will serve you well – you find it very hard to stay in one place for very long and value a wide range of experiences and knowledge.

Keep transcribing – you are right in believing that finishing the book will "break the wall," – that pattern that for many lifetimes has prevented you from attaining your true potential! We assure you, once this lesson is completed, the proverbial dam will break and everything will become so much easier. The daily yoga practice, the piano lessons, all will fall into place once this lesson is achieved. We believe that you can indeed finish during this trip to visit your father: just keep working and give yourself this gift. Sleep now, and we will give you more tomorrow.

JULY 29, 2016
AM, PETERSHAM, MASSACHUSETTS

Archangel Michael:

Good morning, Beloved – such is the measure of the days you are destined for: writing, seeing and traveling, and taking lovely photos! Your mission is to Awaken – and beauty is one of the best ways to get people's attention. We do not speak of the shallow Hollywood version of beauty, but rather the simple appreciation of a flower, the feel of cool breeze against your skin, or the taste of a ripe peach. When a person is fully immersed in such, her eyes open, her mind expands – she is in the glorious Now. She learns what it feels like to breathe and to relax – this is the foundation of being Awake. Another aspect: when one is awake, the mind is quiet, for it is impossible to be fully in the Now and simultaneously to worry about bills or jobs. For one is *fear* and one is *love,* and the two cannot coexist.

JULY 31, 2016
PM (LATE), PETERSHAM, MASSACHUSETTS

Archangel Michael:

Blessed evening to you, Beloved! In a few short minutes it will be your birthday, and the beginning of a new year for you. You will be 46! ($4 + 6 = 10 = 1 + 0 = 1$ (beginning and unity consciousness)!)

We strongly urge you to finish the manuscript – this is the steppingstone upon which everything else depends. We know you have many other demands upon your time, and We suggest that you use your free will now to choose some typing! (Laughter) Sleep well – you have an upgrade tonight!

AUGUST 2, 2016
PM, UNIVERSITY OF CONNECTICUT

Archangel Michael:

Greetings, Beloved – it's been a long time since you woke up feeling that groggy and nauseated, has it not? It was the cake: concentrated sugar is the culprit – and too little sleep.

We wish today to address the book and where it should end. You were right to begin editing now instead of writing further: the book ends essentially with the second notebook. There is still work to do on the first book, but we feel your excitement about the second book! We do caution you – the first book must be finished first (laughter) – We know how excited you get at the start of things, so We will work with you to "finish first things first." But yes, there is another book already in these journals!

Michele D. Baker

"In but the space of a heartbeat there is room and opportunity for redemption."
— Archangel Gabriel

58 Michele D. Baker

Enjoy the next days (month) as they will be the last ones you spend doing other work! Very soon your financial abundance will roll in – you're already experiencing so many other types of abundance, and the frozen energy called "money" comes next. We will give you guidance on spending it if you wish!

We also urge you to put back on your plate and bring back to consciousness those items which you want to increase or multiply. For example, We know you often think about a regular yoga practice and learning piano. Bring those back to the "front burner" as now is the time to cultivate new habits, inform new strands, create different processes: to *begin*. We will help you.

AUGUST 17, 2016
AM, HOME

Archangel Michael:

Welcome back, Beloved – our smooth transition from tongue to pen is a joy for Us as well – We missed you! – although it feels strange for Us to say, since We are *never* separate from you.

The sadness you feel when watching the television show "Outlander" is an issue with many facets. You yearn for what you perceive to be a romantic former time. This is to some extent true, but the reality was a harsh climate, hard work, lack of hygiene and early death for many. You also connect deeply with the love between the main characters Jamie and Claire: this sadness is the recognition of memory. You have known this great love and you ache to feel it again. *This is a gift, Beloved!* If you were here alone on Earth, you would not have these feelings – you would not yearn for the connection created when you discover and reconnect with your own Soul's twin.

This journey you and all humans are on is about reconnection: reconnecting the DNA, reconnecting to your experience and memory of a unified Universe (as opposed to a dualistic one), reconnecting to your Divinity, reconnecting to your power as a co-creator of the Universe and your destiny as a master.

We suggest you get out more – part of your task is to feel and heal, which is much harder at home alone. Do not worry about your mother; she is on her own path and will be just fine. Sleep well, Beloved – We will speak again later.

Archangel Michael:

Dearest One, We are so pleased to speak to you and hear your thoughts. We feel your discomfort and disquiet, but We assure you that never do you disappoint Us when you use your own free will *not* to write, although for you to write twice daily is Our own preference.

We hear your questions: when will you feel better? When will the books be published? When will your life *begin*? We say to you: Now! Your life is so very different from it was this time last summer – working both a full and a part time job – and now, working two very part time jobs and with the very real promise and prospect of a career as a writer here in your lap! What will you do with all your free time? (You'll have no more excuses for missing yoga and piano lessons, that's for sure!) (Laughter)

We can also joyously tell you that the authors whom you have admired will become colleagues and even friends, especially Matt Kahn and Martha Beck. These and other enlightened souls are part of your tribe, and as such they are very much looking forward to meeting you, too! Your circle of artists and creative minds will soon expand a very great deal.

Regarding your proposed trip and your mother's broken car, We can only say that nothing less would have kept you here, where you are urgently needed to balance the energies. Your mother also needed to stay away from Northern Illinois, as that vibration is now unhealthy for her and to you, as well, Beloved. If you go visit your family there, you must take special care, as the energy buildup there is at a critical mass and will soon erupt and recalibrate into a more even wave form. But now this is a dangerous place – We use this word advisedly – for intuitive people and empaths like you and your mother and We urge you to stay away for a few months until that energy has been fully assimilated there. We feel your distress, as We rarely speak in this manner, but your physical health would be affected. Please believe Us, Beloved – you can send love and healing, but you must do so for now from a distance. Many of the other members of your family are not at the same energetic space, and they will ride the wave, but your vibration would lower there to such a level as to cause serious illness. Better to "love them from afar" for now.

We love you so much and are so proud of you – sleep well!

AUGUST 22, 2016
PM, HOME

Archangel Michael:

Good evening, Beloved One! Thus it is with all things: something must end so something else may begin. The energy transfer is completed only upon "receipt" of the "old" and so acts as fuel or raw material for the new.

Book Two is nearing completion: but you must work on it to finish the task. Only then can the next steps occur. We feel your impatience but point only to the task at hand before you. You may speed up or slow down the process as much as you would like – this is the nature of free will.

You will sell many books and open many hearts, Beloved! This We have seen, and it is so. We urge you to "get on with it" and bring to reality that life of which you have long dreamed! We will wake you up early – get up and type, work on the book. You are so close to achieving your goal: let nothing stop you now. We love you so much.

Sleep now, and We will speak again tomorrow.

AUGUST 25, 2016
PM, HOME

Archangel Michael:

Good evening, Beloved – We are pleased that you worked on the book today! If you spend some time tomorrow, you should finish, and be ready for the next step.

We hear your acceptance of your power and the gratitude for coming abundance. We also feel your delight at the twin flame reconnection and are eager for this reconnection to manifest. This is your birthright and your promise from Us, who helped you to create the Interlife plan for this most magnificent lifetime. We applaud you! Go and rest, and We will speak again tomorrow.

AUGUST 28, 2016
PM, HOME

Archangel Michael:

Wonderful evening to you, Beloved! You have taken a good first step into the world that includes baring these Messages – a vital part of you – to an "outsider." Your bravery is to be commended! We know you fear having others think you are lying, or crazy or flaky or a conspiracy nut. But We assure you, those responses will be few and far between, for people are hungry for the Truth and for explanations of the events they cannot conceive of: even when those explanations may seem at first fantastical.

You are very close, Beloved – a very, very short "time" stands between you and the new life you've waited for. Congratulations! Sleep now, but We must speak again tomorrow.

AUGUST 31, 2016
PM, HOME

Archangel Michael:

Greetings, Beloved! We wish to give you the final details about the book: add in the quotes you found and finish the resources and additional reading. Your acknowledgement section will grow with the editing process, so don't worry too much about that being unfinished. Your publisher awaits!

We were pleased to see you energized by your work discussions today, and much good information was brought to the forefront. However, if the probabilities remain as they now are, neither you nor your colleague Audrey will be there next summer to implement them: for sure you will not be there, and she will most likely not be there. Other pathways and ventures await you, Beloved – most related to book signings, travel and the start of a public speaking career. Clearly, this will keep you very busy, as will the writing and editing of Book Two, which you have already begun in this notebook! By the time Book One is translated into other languages, Book Two will be well on its way. Think ahead about the associated pieces: video, audio, CDs, podcasts – they must be part of the total package you provide so as many as possible have access to these Messages. We do not know yet if you will take up doing classes as many speakers have done, but you may elect to expound upon topics We have enumerated: Love, Time, Truth, Death,

Gratitude Game #6

FABULOUS ME FILES

This game takes some time to set up, but once you do, it can be a life-changer.

From now on, when you get a **wonderful email** or a kind **birthday card,** earn a **certificate of achievement,** get a **good review,** win a **trophy** (or anything else that makes you feel glad), put a copy (or a photo of it) into a file folder called **"Fabulous Me!"** on your laptop or desk drawer. When you're feeling uncertain or stuck, pull out the file, grab a random item, and remember how awesome you really are!

(Bonus points for making a version of this for your spouse, children, best friend or even Aunt Flossie.)

P.S. A pretty glass jar or vase filled with dozens of mini, handwritten gratitude notes and tied with a red ribbon makes a great Valentine's gift.

Michele D. Baker

Discernment, etc. You must decide if such work appeals to you now – We know that as a teacher you are more than capable of such lessons, but is it your will to go down the education path again? This is a decision which you must make: let's call it an "optional extra." It would increase the ability of many to assimilate the lessons, but it would also require much time, and you may choose whether or not to fulfill that task.

The spa is still a strong probability and that may be of more interest to you in the long term, rather than educational offerings. If you do the spa, there are many new and exciting opportunities We can elucidate, including new ways to clean water, charge water, use water as a healing tool, and others. Since We know so strongly of your love for beauty and pampering, this pathway may be of the most interest. Sleep well!

SEPTEMBER 3, 2016
PM, HOME

Archangel Michael:

Greetings, Dear One, from all your Team and your Beloveds here in spirit! We applaud you and your diligence to the books and say to you that "it is finished," as the acknowledgements and index will be finished by the publisher. Feel gratitude now, Beloved! This is the signal and the sign you've been waiting for: the message to the Universe for the next step will fall into place ahead of you.

We are so excited and proud – there is much and joy in here in the Celestial Realms and among those beings of the Light that have assisted and labored with you in the creation of these books. There is much gladness as this belongs to all of Us as well, although as Our mouthpiece you will get the tangible benefits! (laughter) We have waited for this day to arrive, Beloved, and We are so very proud!

Walk now in expectation of the next steps being shown to you and fulfilled in their due course. Sleep now, and dream of brighter skies and all the rewards that come with the job well done!

SEPTEMBER 6, 2016
AM, Home

Archangel Michael:

Thank you for waking up to write early, beloved! We are pleased and proud at your swift progress toward this next phase, and very pleased that you correctly read Our Frank's message.

There is so much to tell you, We hardly know where to begin! This is a very special time of year, and the new moon brought a great flood and rush of healing energy which was felt by all and perceived for its true nature by many. There is a real shift going on at this time, with pieces going first one way, then another. We know you will understand this, Beloved, as your clarity of vision has increased so very much in recent months. It is a joy to see and to welcome sight – a sight for sore eyes! We here in the Celestial Realms are often excited in this way when someone "gets it" and a corner is turned. Such is Our excitement now at this moment in history. All things turn in favor of the Light!

Your fear of what others will say when they read the books is understandable but unnecessary, Beloved. Even the most closed-minded humans have at least *heard* of the things mentioned in the books, although they would be disinclined to believe. (It is not as if a caveman were presented with an airplane!) Each person must exercise his own free will to decide whether or not he will use his eyes to see and his ears to hear the Truth about the world – that lies and systems have been long used to pull a blanket of darkness across your minds and keep your spirits chained to small lives and fevered dreams. The birthright of every being is such amazing abundance – why would anyone settle for less?

In this Now, this day, this moment, rejoice in all that has changed in the short time since you began the book projects. Although as you well know "time" does not exist, this sentence does mean so much to you! Since last summer, you have completely upgraded your DNA to 13 active strands, quit your full-time job, written a book, transformed your health by eliminating sugar, reconnected with several old friends, and finished a task that We promised would permanently end the cycle of blockage. That's quite a lot, is it not? We are pleased you now see the full magnitude of all you have accomplished in service to the light, and the short timeframe in which it has occurred. Perhaps now you see a "valid" reason for Our pleasure!

Take time today to be in this bliss, Beloved One. You have earned it. We will speak again.

Michele D. Baker

SEPTEMBER 7, 2016
PM, HOME

Archangel Michael:

Good evening to you, Beloved and *yes,* it is good to go back and reread the things you previously wrote – you realized this evening that the invitation to help type the book was less than three months ago. It was the fourth of July when you got your notebook back and began typing in earnest – that was only two months ago. Since then, you've typed and edited the first draft, and – thanks to impulsed guidance – to contact Our Frank, you've already embarked on the next step: sending copies out for comments. Can you see how much has happened in just eight weeks?

We have a special assignment for you in Dallas. Go say hello in person to Matt Kahn: he is a member of your tribe, and he will recognize you as such. See what wonderful things become of it! Sleep well, Beloved and we will speak again, perhaps in the morning.

SEPTEMBER 9, 2016
PM, DALLAS

Archangel Michael:

So, Beloved, you are feeling the love all around you now, yes? And seeing how the love potentials from last night's Matt Kahn program carried over throughout today? See how easy it is to live in the midst of synchronicity and harmony? We knew you would immediately understand this Message: that all proceeds from the Light, and all *is* Light. What an extraordinary way to go through existence – not wanting, not expecting, not fearing, not judging – just synchronicity and gratitude, and surrounded by smiling people glad to be a part of your journey.

We are so proud of you for asking Isaac outright about his beliefs – that took a lot of courage, as it is often hard to know where one's individual beliefs lie, and if you offend, there is awkwardness thereafter. What a relief for you, too; now, you can talk without editing! There is much joy in finding "kindred spirits." Rest now, Beloved – We feel you are weary. We will speak again.

Gratitude Game #7

NAME THE SKY

Expand your vocabulary to make your gratitude even more powerful.

NAME THE SKY
Is it a "blue sky with white puffy clouds"? Or could it be that "the majestic indigo heavens expand to fill my vision, a shimmering blanket of black velvet sprinkled with diamond stars"?

SYNONYM SALAD
Jazz up your internal gratitude language by using synonyms and adding lots of detail. For example, in your "request" for a new car, you might say, "I'm so grateful for my brand-new candy apple red Corvette with ebony leather seats, sun roof, and personalized tag: HOTCAR1."

DESCRIBE A WELL-LOVED PERSON OR OBJECT
Works well during your morning toothbrushing and face-washing time (see Gratitude Game #5). "My oval face is blessed with flawless caramel skin and blue eyes the color of a Robin's egg."

Michele D. Baker

Archangel Michael:

Good morning, Beloved! We know you had a wonderful night last night, and we applaud your willingness to share so much important information with your friends. They are both wonderful people whose energy is high and ever ready for more love-light. These two souls have incarnated again together to enjoy a lifetime, but also to experience the relative disapproval of people around them, forcing them to lean on each other. This is wise and good, as they can be stronger together, and happiest if they learn to stand in their power, their love-light and united in compassion.

Our Isaac is also such a one and is very precious to you. His presence serves to remind that there are indeed men who are caretakers and who pay attention (Wayne is another such). Fear not, Beloved, Isaac's "One" also approaches in due course! There is much joy for Us in telling you that these people that you love so much have joy in their futures! Of course, they may use their free will to choose another path, but we strongly feel the vast potentials that they will Awaken enough to experience and appreciate true bliss.

Regarding 9/11: there will be low energies out and about today, most masquerading as "memorial" plans to honor the "victims" of the September 11th "disaster." We rarely use so many "quotes," Beloved, so We know you will soon catch Our meaning!

Yes, the September 11th attacks were orchestrated quite deliberately and intricately by your government, with the full cooperation of the highest levels of each branch, to create a need to further "fight terrorism." Those attacks were a 3D betrayal of all that most beings hold dear but remember – there is always another side to every story, and even seemingly-evil deeds fall somewhere on the spectrum of Love. Granted, some actions carry but a mere wisp of a spark, but since Love Is All, nothing can be outside it. Constantly We are beaming love-light to those beings living low in the Light, and there are many opportunities for them to rejoin their comrades in higher frequencies.

In illustration, reference the animated movie "Monsters, Inc.," about a group of monsters scaring children to collect their fearful screams for energy and discovering that children's laughter is 1,000 times more powerful!

Also regarding 9/11: there are those who know the Truth about the events on those days, and who have been suppressed by governments to keep quiet. Soon the silence will end, Beloved, for all eventually comes to light (delighted laughter) and nothing ever remains truly hidden. Go and feel how the day feels and remember to wrap yourself in a giant bubble of light – those outside this house may need a little boost. We shall speak again tonight.

LATER THAT DAY

Archangel Michael:

Quiet today, yes, Beloved? There were few people making 9/11 memorials. This is the nature of the 3D human mind – it forgets so quickly! – but calmness is always a blessing. Sleep now and we will speak again tomorrow.

SEPTEMBER 20, 2016
PM, HOME

Archangel Michael:

And so it is, Beloved One, that We come again to you and speak in this written form! Our Lelon has given you much new information. Indeed, the confirmation from your astrological chart, of Mercury in Leo, is a sure sign that you were born to be a communicator, specifically a writer! The further knowledge – that you embody an aspect of Mary the Magdalene – your fascination with her story is now clear, yes? This is good news, and the pieces come together and form a beautiful tapestry for your life. This is a blessing! We are so proud that these strands of DNA have "come online" and are now active, for this is the step you are on, Beloved. The DNA is waking up, and new memories, new lifetimes, new skills and abilities are now available to you as this place is reached. As you continue your spiritual quest/journey the spiral will continue upward and more and more "secrets" will unlock and be made available to you. We say "secrets" because the 3D plane (in reality, the 3D/5D plane) is full of hidden information that can only be accessed when the correct frequency is achieved. We have said many times before that everything in the Universe has a vibration and you must "tune" to it to activate it or "go" there. This is true of All That Is, Beloved, even knowledge. As you continue upward, more knowledge will be available, and faster, for the spiral's circuits become shorter and shorter but still contain the same "amount" of wisdom as in the larger circuits.

We thrill to the challenges you have overcome so far, and We honor the hard work you have done. We are excited even here, Beloved, to see these Messages coming together so quickly into books. We felt your surprise when you realized the process that had felt so long was really only eight weeks! Remember, "time" is malleable and flexible! This is a wonderful practical example of just that concept.

Be at peace about Wayne, Beloved. He works at his own pace and is still a human _doing_ (as opposed to a human _being_), but even now, the seeds are being planted. Watch for that relationship to bear wonderful friendship fruit.

Your own beloved approaches as well, as he is part of the book publishing process. You will know him instantly from his eyes! We know this news both pleases and scares you. That's OK! All is happening in Divine Right Timing, so all is perfect. Be still and in gratitude and simply allow. Good night for now!

SEPTEMBER 21, 2016
PM, HOME

Archangel Michael:

Greetings, Beloved and a blessed night to you! We have much to tell you this evening.

Edward is living now a more full and rich life, but he still does things with the aim to please others. Such is the dove hunting he does tonight. He is not interested in dove hunting as such, but he goes along with the crowd. You can do nothing more for this beloved Soul except to send him Love-Light. He misses you because he is lonely and would seek your company as a panacea instead of creating his own contentment and comfort; he must learn to do this for himself.

Wayne heeded your words and opened the book manuscript you sent him, although he did not read it in its entirety. He is amazed and overwhelmed by its messages, but will wait until later to give you his feedback. He did not, as you suggested, use the "find" feature to skip through to the parts about himself.

The books are anchoring firmly in 3D/5D space and will soon be reality. Your tribe has had many good comments for you which will strengthen the books' readability. Also, each person who loves and accepts these works adds his or her own Love-Light to them and makes the whole stronger. This is good! We are pleased that so many beloved friends agreed to read and comment. This is a blessing to you, Beloved. The collaborative nature of the Message is reflected in the books. Our Marcie will have especially good comments.

Sleep now and spend some time with Us tomorrow!

SEPTEMBER 22, 2016
AM, HATTIESBURG, MISSISSIPPI

Archangel Michael:

Greetings and salutations, Beloved One! We greet you this morning with much enthusiasm and excitement for the day ahead with Marcie. She has much wisdom to contribute to the books and to your life, so this is a wonderful opportunity to spend time in both friendship and spiritual reflection. We here in the higher realms do love this form of "two-fer," you know!

We feel your mind wandering, so go and do your other work. We will speak again later.

SEPTEMBER 26, 2016
PM, HOME

Archangel Michael:

Hello, Beloved – We are so pleased you received our gift! The beautiful being you know as Kaisha is one of Ours: a half-angel hybrid whose mission it is to carry messages from the Celestial Realms to the Earth plane. Your Soulmate's essence did indeed come through her last night to say hello and to assure you that he is waiting for you as impatiently as you await him. The being you call Kaisha has a deep heart and spirit connection to this realm and that healing heart energy called "Love-Light," "compassion," or simply "Love" is her gift to the 3D/5D plane and her mission at this juncture. Like you and your writing, which touches and spreads Love, so, too does Kaisha's gift. She touches beings with her pure spirit and wakes them up or spurs them to the next level. You could call what she does spirit healing: it is no accident she was a nurse who brought new life into the world, nor was it a coincidence that she then pursued healing via therapeutic massage and energy work. These were necessary steppingstones to the place she is going: a "healer for hire" – someone you can call on to fix you up! We feel your frustration with this term, Beloved. Let Us give some more detail.

Kaisha's mission is to go where she is needed and give Universal healing energy. She has a good sense of this mission already, but she does not know if she can sustain the frozen energy called "money" by doing this work. *She can!* She will always have exactly what she needs to get where she needs to go. This will be a life that to outsiders looks like a hand-to-mouth existence, but in reality, it is a constant flow of abundance in each moment. There does not need to be "storage" or "savings," because manna falls from Heaven each day upon her to fulfill her every need. She is always taken care of in the moment.

Your suggestion to her to call herself a "life coach" was a good one but is too small for what she does. Just as she allowed her physical vehicle to be taken over by your Soulmate to bring you a few minutes of joy, so is the mission she carries out with her whole being. She cannot recommend diet and exercise when what that person really needs is an "instant conversion" or a "kick start" – a dose of the same joy you felt that night. She will be fine...

Sleep well, and we will speak again!

OCTOBER 1, 2016
PM, HOME

Archangel Michael:

Greetings, Beloved! There is much to say this evening, and We know you are hurting, so We will come straight to the point.

Our Lelon is going through a major transition. The move to Hawaii is similar in nature to your finishing the first book – a major roadblock about to be crashed through and overcome, and all that lies beyond is finally at hand. This is a huge shift for him and for you and there is much to explain, and more to add to what you already know. Lelon loves you, and he genuinely wants you to be happy and successful. He feels as though you are family: as he said, he has very few friends, but those he does have are precious to him. In many ways he views you as a younger sister, or even a daughter (you have been father and daughter before).

Too, his cherished reputation has been tarnished in previous incarnations, and some of that residual anger is spilling over on to you, Beloved. He is expecting you to "stab him in the back" as others have done before, both literally and figuratively. The fact that you did nothing to provoke his outburst is proof of his deep-seated fear that it will happen again. Renee told you truly – Lelon was telling you his deepest fears: to be publicly maligned and discredited, "stabbed in the back," and left alone... again. This aspect of Lelon – that of the Spiritual Warrior – causes him to see things in very black and white terms. He is a Warrior of the Light, and his assertion that his spiritual life is more important than friendship is a coping skill in case you turn out to be yet another disappointment. He believes in his mission here much more than you currently understand, Beloved.

This man is important in your life, Beloved, and you must show him how much. You must also tell him how much his words hurt you: words that were not earned, but rather a reflection of his own fear. You will know this lighted being for much longer, so value this unpleasant experience as a dear Soul crying out for you to help. "Whatever arises, love that."

Now rest. You will awaken refreshed. We love you so much!

OCTOBER 2, 2016
PM, HOME

Archangel Michael:

Greetings, Beloved and good night to you! We come to you this evening with the answers you requested about the current and upcoming Earth changes. Aha! You have discovered another facet of our conversations: you can guide to some extent the context and the direction of the words We send! There will always be things We wish to share, but this is meant to be a partnership, a dialogue, a discussion, so of course you should do your part and ask questions or request specific information.

The phase Gaia is in is an early third phase/5D construct of mortal time. Let Us explain. There have been two prior phases: the original construct, which was, for lack of better and more precise terminology, perfect. Phase One was unity consciousness, and beings on your planet understood their position in the greater whole and were pleased to live within those boundaries. Then came "the fall" which was the beginning of Phase Two. Humans' DNA was downgraded, and they forgot, temporarily (although it felt permanent), their connection to the God-Source/All That Is. They began to experience duality, a perceived separateness, which of course, is false, as there is nowhere to be that is not part of All That Is. That was amnesia, a forgetting of the Divine Birthright and the powers that accompany it. As of 1948, you have now entered Phase Three, a resurgence of unity consciousness, coincidental to the reconnection of the other 11 DNA strands.

We also gave the qualifier "3D/5D," which follows along with these phases. 3D is a dualistic construct, but which to many humans feels like reality. It is *real* but not *reality*. People's minds and expectations make it real insofar as they experience 3D as their reality, but the Truth, the Reality, is a 5D and higher way of perceiving the Universe, and existing and thriving within it. The vast majority of humans still exist in this rapidly vanishing 3D plane, but they are quickly Awakening, and when they begin to experience life on the 5D plane, they much prefer it (although some fear they died without knowing and have entered heaven).

As 3D makes way for 5D, Earth changes will accelerate. These include extreme weather conditions, as the earth tries to balance deserts and ice caps; solar storms that inundate earth with massive radiation; extinction of animal and plant species (they have completed their 3D incarnations); and many human system changes.

"Writing gratitude letters helps... even if you don't send them."
— Dr. Brown & Dr. Wong

Michele D. Baker

We have spoken of a few of these system changes in greater detail: human "sickness" – the physical body adjusts to the new frequency; financial crisis – the frozen energy system called money serves only the very few and must be replaced with a more equitable system; education failures – schools and colleges cannot prop up the failing systems much longer; government – new leaders await the day very soon when their ethical leadership will run countries with the consent of the governed; religions that teach of sin and separateness from God will phase out as humans realize they are each sparks of Divinity temporarily residing in a human shell.

There are many more changes to discuss, Beloved, but these are enough examples for now. The important thing to remember is that all is happening for the ascension of humans into *Homo galacticus*: fully actualized, Awake hue-man beings capable of using their divine birthright powers as part of a just society in harmony with Gaia. The Light is winning and shall prevail!

Sleep now and let's talk tomorrow. Goodnight.

OCTOBER 3, 2016
PM, HOME

Archangel Michael:

Hello, Beloved, from the Celestial Realms and your Crew! We are so very pleased that Our Iyana gave you such powerful feedback this afternoon. Her input is valuable, and her counsel is wise. We foresee this lighted being in your pathway for many years to come. We also want to reassure you that Lelon is still your friend. You must learn a practical lesson, "whatever arises, love that!" and when it is hurting, they need more love, not less. You have a suspicious nature, Beloved. This is a result of insecurity as a result of your past, but the current pattern bears Us out: all is well, and people do love you. The lessons you came here to embody and learn include giving others the credit and the opportunity to have a second chance. You must give this chance with your whole heart and allow someone who spoke his truth the honor of accepting that truth, even if you did not like what was being said. This is vital, for many people are scorned for speaking their truths, and We do not wish you to be one of these, Beloved.

We hear you have some questions:

Q: Will I go to Egypt for Christmas this year?

A: The potentials are strong, but we cannot say with certainty, as there are many pieces of the puzzle in motion at this time. We are leaning toward no. Because the book might be in progress at that time; please make the updates and call your publisher.

Good night, and sleep well, Dear One!

OCTOBER 5, 2016
PM, TUPELO

Archangel Michael:

Hello and greetings this fine evening, Beloved One! We know you are tired from the day's exertions, but We wish to tell you a few items before you sleep.

First, the book you are reading is, of course, put in your path to let you see the ever-important Divine Masculine perspective. If Divine Feminine is to flourish, it must be in balance with the Divine Masculine. These lighted souls of the Divine Masculine desire greatly to partner with you as the Goddess you are, but the "bad reputation" men now have was earned by men and women who did not embody traits of either the Divine Masculine or Feminine. There is much to be gained from such a partnership, and this book will help you on your quest to have an ever-better relationship with men; all men, including your father, brother, uncles, co-workers, friends, and your Soul Mate, who is approaching fast.

Sleep now, and We shall speak again tomorrow.

OCTOBER 19, 2016
PM, HOME

Archangel Michael:

Ahhh, Beloved, We have missed you! We are excited for you to use the new lapis lazuli pendulum your just purchased. It is a powerful transmitter and this stone will certainly enhance our ability to communicate effectively.

We have felt your stress this past week, and We wish to address a few items quickly before you sleep well tonight: Renee is shifting DNA to six strands; this is the root cause of her "illnesses," and they will dissipate on their own in a few weeks. She must simply wait: a miracle cure is coming! There is a lot of energy shifting now, especially the last few days with the full moon, and many are feeling the shift, although they do not know what is happening.

As for you, go now and rest. We will speak again.

"Gratitude unshackles us from toxic emotions."
- Dr. Brown & Dr. Wong

Michele D. Baker

OCTOBER 20, 2016
PM, HOME

Archangel Michael:

Greetings, Beloved, from your Celestial Team. We are so pleased your self-imposed hiatus of speaking with Us has ended. There is much still to tell you, and much yet to do to birth this one of our many joint books.

We again urge you to complete the edits to the book so your publisher can find you. We know you think you need to do the online course, and you may, if you wish. Do that, but in truth, Beloved, there is no need. You already have all the knowledge you need to bring this project into the 3D physical Earth plane, and your experience will be much different from other authors'. We have told you this before, and it remains true. The steps you take now are divinely guided and part of the plan you made in the Interlife, and part of the Divine Record of this lifetime in the Akashic Records.

We hear your question: how could something already be in the Akashic Records if it has not yet occurred? *Because time is not linear, Beloved!* Some things are karmic, predetermined, and as set in stone as is possible to be in a free will universe. These books are some of those things – the only holdup right now is *you.*

We are so pleased that Lelon told you of your planetary alignment pointing to the books. It is indeed an ingrained part of your psyche to create in this way. When he told you of the positions of the many planets at the time of your birth, and how they pointed to writing as a career, it was so joyful to feel your relief and recognition. You are truly destined to be a writer, and We thrill to the emotional and physical changes that show that you have received that information and assimilated it. It is such a wonderment to you, but a real pleasure for Us as well!

Sleep now, and we will speak again.

OCTOBER 25, 2016
PM, HOME

Archangel Michael:

Good evening and hello, Beloved; We are so glad to speak with you this evening! We are excited at the progress you are making, keeping your energy high and keeping moving is the key, as you now clearly see. You are also clearly receiving Our messages to reduce or eliminate meat from your diet, one step at a time. Also, and you know this Beloved, you must eliminate sugar. This is bad for you specifically as it interferes with the hormone production within your new DNA structure.

We are also pleased to tell you and confirm that Renee is on the mend. Her physical symptoms are indeed those of Ascension, a "sickness" that has no specific 3D caused discernible by doctors *because there is no 3D cause.* This is a frequency shift mismatch and is temporary. She must understand the symptoms. (She could read your manuscript if you wish.)

On that note, please make time tomorrow to finish the edits. Your publisher is awaiting. Sleep well and we will speak again tomorrow.

OCTOBER 26, 2016
PM, HOME

Archangel Michael:

Hello, Beloved One. We immediately feel your distress at not working today on the book. It is OK! But you must decide, what is your priority? The life you want, or the life you now have? Because, as you know, your focus determines your energy level toward your goals. If the projects you choose for yourself take low priority, they won't get the attention they deserve and need to get done. This is of course fine (We give no judgement here), but if your goal is the book and to be a writer, that is where your attention must live. You know this.

Sleep well and try to get some editing done tomorrow. We will speak again.

NOVEMBER 7, 2016
PM, HOME

Archangel Michael:

Good evening, Beloved, We have missed you! The forces of the Dark have many subtle ways of keeping lightworkers down, and doubt and anger are two of the most insidious and powerful. Your irritation this past week was in part a warning signal from Us that you'd "strayed from your path [of writing]," and a clear indication of influence of the Dark. You lose your power when you feel your concentration has been lost. Of course, you never *really* lose the connection, but the doubt and fear cause you to *think* you've lost the connection. And as you well know, discontent and fear breed confusion, frustration and anger. Thank you for asking Us to intervene, as We cannot do so without your request and approval. Now is a good time to include the Manifestation Command:

> *I, (your full name), Extension of and Co-Creator with the Divine, Eternal Love-Light Source of All Existence and the Holy Spirit of the Christed Light, in the name of the Archangels Michael, Uriel, Gabriel, Raphael and the entire hierarchy of the Archangels, Angels, Powers, Principalities and Dominions of the Christed Light Forces, do now command that (name of recipient) yields to the Will of the Highest Good for (your full name).*
>
> *All other Will, not of the Christed Light, backfires and binds (name of recipient) and the anti-Christed source from which it comes, for the Highest Good, whatever that may be. So it is spoken, so it is done, and so it is! (clap three times)*

[Author's Note: here is one example of the Command as I would use it, with my usual changes, as a manifestation of an event instead of as a backfire/binding. I recommend doing the "Ground/Center/Shield Gratitude Game" (see page 6) to get mentally and spiritually prepared for this Command.]

> I, Michele Dawn Baker, a being high in the Christed light and a member of the Celestial team of the Archangel Michael, and in the name of the divine, eternal Love-Light Source of All Existence, and in the name of the archangels Michael, Uriel, Raphael, and Gabriel and the entire hierarchy of archangels, angels, powers, principalities, and dominions of the Christed Light forces, I do now will and command that the current Book, "Attitude of Gratitude: In Service to the Light Book Two" is manifested into 3D/5D now, and any disruptions, diversions, doubt, or other tricks of the Dark are immediately nullified and canceled painlessly, effortlessly, in all dimensions, in all directions and in all timelines. I command this in the name of the Christed Light forces, for the highest good of all involved. *(Clap three times)* I speak it, I Will it, I Command it and so it is.

NOVEMBER 7, 2016
LATER, HOME

Archangel Michael:

We are glad to facilitate a trip to Egypt for you, beloved and indeed, miracles will occur on this trip, for it is an important step on this journey, your first trip to your past home while completely awake and with all 13 strands on and activated! You will feel much there, more than ever before. Spend some time with your beloved Sphinx, as She is your guide there.

Tomorrow is a new day, so "pay yourself first" and make yourself your first priority. We love you and are so proud of you!

NOVEMBER 8, 2016
PM, HOME

Archangel Michael:

So, Beloved, the election fantasy continues! The gameshow aspects you noted in the news coverage of the U.S. presidential election are an apt description of the "game" humans are playing at this time with your world. Left versus Right. Liberal versus Conservative. Red versus Blue. All are artificial constructs meant to separate you from your fellow travelers toward the Light. The political process is controlled entirely by dark forces, but in the end, all things serve the Light. Their hold is crumbling, and very soon they will have no more hold at all. They struggle to keep in power those politicians whose motives can be bought for money or favors, but beings of the Light and with pure intent continue to enter the political realm and win! This is as it should be, Beloved – systems that work for everyone involved and which respect the dignity of people and of Mother Earth/Gaia.

Sleep now Little One. When you awaken, there will be a new female president of the United States, the first in your history!

Gratitude Game #8

TURN YOUR FROWN UPSIDE DOWN

I have used this game many times to pull me out of a blue funk, road rage, or even blazing anger. It always feels strange at first, but keep it up. After a minute or two, your body begins to assimilate the new message. You might even feel your mood shift from anger, to irritation, to alright, and finally to contentment.

Begin with simple gratitudes like "I'm so grateful I'm breathing," "I'm grateful for Grandma's chocolate chip cookies," and "I'm grateful for Rover and Fido."

Keep talking nonstop, beginning each new sentence with "I'm grateful that..." or "I'm so grateful for..." Keep talking until you feel better (however you define that).

Even if some of the gratitudes are nonsense, this Game should quickly improve your mood. (Don't worry about repeating yourself: I've had great results from saying, "I'm grateful for kittens and rainbows" 50 times, and I ended up grinning.)

Michele D. Baker

NOVEMBER 10, 2016
PM, HOME

Archangel Michael:

A blessed evening to you, Dear One, and we feel your confusion at the outcome of the presidential election! The potentials shifted very fast and quite unexpectedly to bring Mr. Trump into power. Two factions of the Illuminati are currently at war with each other and fighting for control of those Souls on the slower end of the Awakened spectrum. (We say "slower end" because the spectrum continues in all directions, and even those Souls taking a "long" time are *on the spectrum*. Where else would they be?) These two factions are squabbling like lost children over what little power remains to be had. They are like piranhas swarming – they have begun to eat each other.

Watch for big changes, Beloved. We encourage you to take a last look though [Book One] before surrendering to sleep tonight. We will take it from here. Good night!

NOVEMBER 14, 2016
PM, HOME

Archangel Michael:

Greetings, Beloved. We are excited to travel with you to Egypt tomorrow! Your guide Ezekiel has overall charge of you while you're on the move, and this capable being will ensure smooth flights and comfortable travel. There will likely be a delay in Paris due to weather, so watch for that.

We are excited at how close you are coming to completion—the dam is chipping away, and soon the flood of "all that comes after" will be a reality on the 3D plane. We feel your growing excitement, and We encourage you again to do/adopt these measures and habits which will aid you in this process: walking outside, yoga, eating less and lighter, avoiding sugar and meat, writing twice a day. Go now and rest. We will speak again.

Michele D. Baker

NOVEMBER 16, 2016
AM, CHARLES DE GAULLE AIRPORT, PARIS

Archangel Michael:

Bonjour, Beloved! We are pleased you received our instructions to go to the lovely lounge, a reflection of the French way, that all travelers deserve a (free) beautiful and quiet place to rest between flights. You are among the first to use this space, and it is for you that it exists, a comfortable and safe space for a "time in-between."

The next part of your journey will go as smoothly as the first, and then you will arrive in Cairo: Habibi will be at the airport to receive you. This is an auspicious time for you all – the beginning of a new era! Take some time to work on the books. We love you so much!

NOVEMBER 22, 2016
EARLY AM, GIZA PLATEAU, EGYPT

Archangel Michael:

Precious morning to you, Beloved One! We are joined today by the energy of the Sphinx – She wishes to communicate with you.

Great Sphinx:

We are the mighty Sphinx from which blessings flow. We watch over all who come to be in Our presence, and We are sacred and holy. Be in our embrace and all shall be healed. All shall be well. We are the Protector of the Light. We are that which has no beginning and no end. There are many secrets which lie within Us. Seek Us and you shall uncover them. Go in peace.

Archangel Michael:

So Beloved, another communication with The Mighty Sphinx. As you already know, She comes from Sirius and was built in her physical body by master craftsmen from that planet. You were there and Her original 3D form bore your face, not unlike the face you have today! She is pleased you are here with Her and She is infusing your DNA with even more healing energy. Indeed, you have had two "upgrades" in the week you have been here. This is why you have been eating and sleeping so little yet have been full of energy: you are vibrating at a much higher level than ever before! Today will be a very full day; you will see much happen as things come together and are assimilated. It will be fun. Go now and come to Us later!

DECEMBER 1, 2016
PM, CAIRO, EGYPT

Archangel Michael:

Hello, Precious One! Thank you for coming to Us tonight before sleeping. We know that you are very tired, so We will make Our message brief.

All things move in your favor now. All is in readiness for the miracle of the book that is your contribution to the world, your promise to your God-self in the life in-between lives. We know that you are tired and excited about this new venture, but please finish. Sleep now; We will speak again.

DECEMBER 13, 2016
PM, HOME

Archangel Michael:

Thank you for coming to Us tonight. Although We are always with you, it gives Us great pleasure to be with you again tonight, Beloved. We have missed your constant presence with Us, and we feel your anxiousness and guilt over the long separations between writings. We do not ever blame or accuse you, Beloved: you do that to yourself! We here in this Realm feel only compassion and love for the many trials you seemingly undergo there in the denser planes. The causes and effects are sometimes far separated, and so there can be a perception of ill luck or poor choices in the short term, when in fact decisions made long ago could be the ultimate catalyst.

We can feel what you are wondering about: What are they talking about? We refer now to the situations and reactions in the United States political realm that led to Donald Trump gaining the presidency. Many in your country do not want, nor welcome, this President. Our Matt Kahn was correct when he said that Mr. Trump is here at this time to shake things up! He is not controllable by the Illuminati powers, and so he is a purer aspect than Hillary Clinton in that sense. He will give many Souls the opportunity to wake up and to realize that _you_ are who you've been waiting for! No longer can your citizens sit back and blame others; they must rise to their own power. President Trump will see to this outcome, and thus fulfill his purpose. Rest now. We will speak more tomorrow.

DECEMBER 14, 2016
PM, HOME

Archangel Michael:

Hello again, Sweet One! We speak to you gladly from Our place here in the Celestial Realms. It is a pleasure to have your attention again, and there is much We wish to discuss.

A solar flare is entering your solar system, a very large one, which is many orders of magnitude larger than any flare your scientists have measured recently. It is, in fact of a similar size, type, and nature to the flare about 20 years ago—the flare which would have engulfed your planet and destroyed it—like that flare, your Team is surrounding the Earth with a protective grid and modulating the flare's wavelength to ameliorate the damage it would cause. Normally such intervention would be beyond the scope of Our ability to intercede in Earth's affairs, but Gaia has requested that We in this Realm assist her, as many of her life forms are not yet sufficiently enlightened to withstand intact such a storm. We, along with members of the Galactic High Council, have agreed to the request and have "installed" a crystalline grid (yes, you are correctly getting the image of an interlocking mesh of snowflakes) to protect Gaia and Earth's physical body from the wave. The technology is easily acquired and quickly installed; this is a common shield for large and small incarnate bodies of all types. It works in tandem with a being's Merkaba and enhances it for even greater protection. (This reminds Us: your most recent "upgrade" did a similar process to your physical body.) This crystalline grid will completely deflect the solar radiation away from Gaia/Earth by literally refracting it simultaneously in thousands of different directions: simple mirror technology! When solar rays hit the grid, they are prismatically refracted in all facets of the snowflake, scattering the radiation harmlessly. No, the "snowflakes" do not "melt" after this process! They are made from a metal called Chromium adamantium which is virtually indestructible, and which is specially tempered for this precise circumstance. Following the solar flare, the grid will simply remain in place, assisting Earth's own ozone layer and providing additional energetic protection as well, in the form of reflecting additional light into Earth's atmosphere, physically en_light_ening her inhabitants even faster.

This is all We wish to tell you this evening. Sleep well!

Gratitude Game #9

SAVOR THE FLAVOR

Sometimes, right in the moment, you have an a-ha moment that feels great: a beautiful song, a delicious meal, a fragrant rosebush, freshly-mown grass... it can be anything that makes you happy.

No matter what else is going on, pause.

Take a moment to truly experience that moment, soak it up and let it sink in. Allow yourself to "savor the flavor."

Michele D. Baker

DECEMBER 20, 2016
PM, Home

Archangel Michael:

Greetings, Beloved One! Your conversation with Jena[4] was indeed divinely inspired. We wanted you to meet this lighted soul and feel her energy! For the moment, join her monthly group. Later, We plan for you to attend an in-person session in New York, but for now, our task for you is one of finishing the books, our number one priority.

Go and let her know. She will appreciate the prompt response. Sleep well, We will speak again tomorrow.

DECEMBER 27, 2016
AM, Home

Archangel Michael:

What a joy it is to speak with you today, Beloved! We greet you from these Realms, which are also feeling the turmoil occurring on the Earth plane.

The election of Donald Trump as president of the United States of America is the result of energy streams and tentacles that built up very quickly during the later parts of his campaign. The more outrageous his speech and behavior, the more he is chastised, which fuels further such behavior. Republicans fear he cannot be controlled; the same fear as the Democrats, ironically; but Mr. Trump is going to surprise everyone. As he is not connected with the Illuminati, he will be able to implement measures that reduce their stranglehold on the world economy. As he believes that he is strong enough to stand up to China, We foresee some movement there. Also, since Mr. Trump openly admires the dictatorial leader Vladimir Putin, there can be partnership between the U.S. and Russia. There is much energy swirling around at this time, too much for any potentials to stand out as yet. We do see a strong potential for this Presidency to knock U.S. citizens out of their complacency and to take that country back. That is all for now.

---

[4] Jena La Flamme, owner of Pleasurable Weight Loss (http://www.pleasurableweightloss.com/) and https://www.jenalaflamme.com/

DECEMBER 28, 2016
PM, HOME

Archangel Michael:

Greetings, Beloved, from your Celestial Family of Light! We wish only to tell you how very much you are loved and cared for. We watch over you with every breath and in every moment you are divinely guided and protected.

Today you are world lost another celebrity, Debbie Reynolds, only one day after losing Carrie Fisher. These two women came in together and left together: partners to the end. They had fulfilled their contracts and so they were able to complete their missions together.

JANUARY 5, 2017
PM, NEW ORLEANS, LOUISIANA

Archangel Michael:

Good evening, Beloved One! We welcome you to this city which you love so much, and We invite you to simply feel how it feels to be here. That is to say that there is no need to force anything or do anything; all is in perfect timing, and all is being taken care of.

We wish to speak to you about the changes that are underway and that have manifested over the last weeks. There was a shift in perception which began when you met with Jena La Flamme by phone and then reread the book "The Queens Code" by Alison A. Armstrong. These two examples of embracing the Divine Feminine are very important for your journey at this time, and the energies coming through right now are supporting your growth into a High Priestess, as evidenced not only by feelings of wanting to know this material, but also by the presence of that tarot card next to the Death/Transformation card in your recent reading, coupled with the lovers card: three major arcana in one area! This is a powerful message from Us to you. Accept the female wisdom We are sending you and embrace your role as a teacher and author. No, Beloved, you will not be doing individual sessions with clients, although you may if you wish. This was Jena's path, but it is not yours.

We see you putting together the various pieces of this puzzle from the many sources and this pleases Us greatly – we are so glad you are a master at synthesizing complex materials from many sources and making it plain for others who follow you. This is a mission and one you are already good at! Your past experience as a teacher was no accident; all were steppingstones to get to this place and time.

It is also no coincidence that all meals you have eaten since the weight loss call with Jena have ended much sooner than you expected; you are learning to really listen to your female animal when she says, "I'm done." Good for you! The exercise also feels good, does it not? We know that you do well when in this situation—having to walk—We will impulse you at home where this may be more difficult.

We feel the fatigue in your hand, so for now, good night. We will speak again.

JANUARY 8, 2017
AM, NEW ORLEANS, LOUISIANA

Archangel Michael:

Good morning, Beloved! The anger pouring out of you is the last remnants of a long-standing anger and disappointment from your childhood. Your father agreed to play an exceedingly difficult role for you; that of abandoner, and he did so, faithfully enduring abandonment by his own father to set up the situation with you. His phone usage now is a small-level continuation of the theme, and the emotions come roaring back to the surface, seemingly at full strength. But step "up," Beloved One, and notice the differences. Are not these new feelings faded versions of those felt previously? Yes, you feel the difference, don't you? At this time of super-quick awakening, those at your level are throwing off the old at a marvelous pace. Soon, this particular well of grief will be empty, and that purging will cease. As each proverbial layer of the onion peels away, a more complete and truthful version (closer to *your* Truth) of you emerges. All is perfect!

We wish to tell you one last thing before you go about your day, Dear One: watch for a sign about your coming books. Do not fear that this most precious gift you give to the world will go unnoticed. It will help many people – this We promise. Enjoy your day!

JANUARY 10, 2017
PM, HOME

Archangel Michael:

Good evening, Dearest One! We feel your tiredness and only wish to assure you that We love and are watching over you. Sleep well and We will speak to you tomorrow.

"Remember to say *thank you.*"
- my Grandma

Michele D. Baker

Archangel Michael:

Good morning, Dearest! It is indeed a pleasure to speak to you this morning! We want to tell you many things: the time has come for even more to be revealed so that our beloved humans can become hue-mans and raise their awareness to a higher level.

This morning We wish to speak of an upcoming event in your 3D Earth, the great energy wave now engulfing your planet. This energy wave originated near the center of your galaxy and spread out in all directions, taking matter in the form of space dust, small meteorites, gases and other compounds with it, all at the speed of light. The vacuum of space allowed this energy and debris to continue moving at the speed of light until much of it was dissipated when it encountered asteroids, planets and other heavenly bodies. But this energy has now reached the vicinity of Earth and has been further strengthened by radiation from the Van Allen belt in your solar system. The combined energy of this wave, the Van Allen belt, and the solar flare from your sun is a powerful force for Earth. This tidal wave of energy will not harm you—on the contrary, it is here to speed up your evolution in a way heretofore only seen in science fiction: in your movies and in your books. This is a wake-up call for many beings on your planet, as there is no stopping such a wave! The shield and grid We spoke of recently is in place and could divert this energy blast, but it is beneficial for the planet to receive it, so the Galactic Council, in cooperation and partnership with Gaia, have agreed not to block the powerful wave, but to allow it to engulf and enlighten the beings of Earth.

In some ways, the wave is an immensely powerful force for mutation. The radiation will literally change DNA and switch on genes that have long been dormant. Scientists on your planet have claimed that human DNA contains a lot of junk DNA, but this is not the case. Rather, these specific genes have not been needed or activated until now.

So what does this mean for you and others? (We hear your question loud and clear, Beloved!) For those who are already walking the path of consciousness, it means an increase in energy and the turning on of genes to do all kinds of things like teleportation, "mind reading," accelerated healing, tapping into the Akashic Records, and more. For those who still choose to sleep, it means the alarm clock has now arrived and is ringing. There can be no more waiting! Everyone remaining incarnate on Earth will now begin, or continue, the ascension process. You have, as a species, "crossed the Rubicon;" there is no going back: only forward, and up!

JANUARY 16, 2017
PM, Home

Archangel Michael:

Hello, Dear One. We are so pleased to speak with you again! Tonight We wish to tie together several ideas which have been floating about at the edge of your awareness, and perhaps a few that will be entirely new. Onward!

The weight you so desperately wish to lose is a manifestation of your fear of lack. You surround yourself with books, food, clothes, friends, jobs. Everything is more than enough. But no matter how much there is, it never satisfies, nor does it fill the need, because the need is emotional. This aspect of your personality is the "addict" from your heritage peeping through in a socially acceptable manner. But it will never, never fulfill you.

Another facet of the same addiction is the need to be liked, to be respected, to be trustworthy and loyal. As Jena was impulsed by Us to tell you, it makes you a slave to others' wishes and denies what you may *yourself* want. There is no harm in being helpful, responsible, or trustworthy. But now you allow others to dictate your life and put yourself last. This is "foolish selfish," Beloved, as the Dalai Lama says.

Finally, your fear of finishing these books is but another facet of the same fear, this time masquerading as a fear of failure. Any one crack in this dam will bring the river of the Real You flooding in. We are here to help and protect you, Beloved! Unplug the cracks, remove your fingers from the dike, and watch the Real You wash away all vestiges of the old fears and the old you. It is no accident that old hurts and resentments about your father are coming to the surface currently. They, too, are aspects of the same issue, what you have called the "boulder you couldn't shift."

Well, Beloved, the shift is here! Live, really live and share that with others. Your mission is to help others awaken by showing them what is possible. You can do this; We implanted Our seeds of this mission well. Open your heart and *see*. Goodnight, and we will speak again.

Michele D. Baker

Archangel Michael:

Beautiful and blessed evening to you, Beloved! As always, We welcome the chance to speak to you and share Our collective wisdom more fully on the 3D plane.

The chaos your world is now experiencing is the final streamers of the breakdown of an old system which no longer serves humanity. Indeed, even when it was "new and shiny," it did not serve you. Rather, it was a system that "pulled the wool over your eyes" and made possible the tension and frustration that grew into the anger and violence you see today. The system is control, and it has many streams, or arms or points of attachment: you know this from the many systems which seem at best, confusing; and at worst, deliberately harmful.

These include educational systems which offer unequal opportunity to some, and which teach outright falsehoods; banking and finance, which create a false sense of lack; the media, which reports only those stories and events which it is allowed to, and ignores others of more value; many governments, which oppress their citizens and give no safety net; medicine, which promotes a "splint and pill" view of health care, and many others.

As these systems collapse, new ones take their places which are a better fit. Education based on learning by creative and fun thought, not rote memorization. Medicine, based on plants and allowing the body to heal itself. New technology, which creates free and clean power and water, and which leaves oil, Earth's blood, inside her body. These systems are in their infancy now but will grow into sustainable underpinnings of a more just society.

Allow these chaotic vestiges to fall away, Beloved, and do not pay too much attention to them. You know it to be true: "what resists, persists." Allow these last fears, the last chaos, and the last poisoned systems to die a natural death. Then build something beautiful to replace them. This is part of your mission to Awaken humans... these new systems!

We love you, and we will speak again.

End of Book Two

Gratitude Game #10

EXPRESS THYSELF

These last three Games were created for teens, but we could all benefit from a little more kindness, so... Have fun!

SAY IT OUT LOUD

Every day, find someone to express your gratitude to: the person who held the elevator door for you, the salesperson who rang you up, your mom for the delicious meal.

PAY IT FORWARD, AKA "Random Acts of Kindness"

There are thousands of small things you can do as "happy" for others: Do the dishes, even if it's your sister's turn. Bring in your neighbor's trash cans from the street. Let somebody pull in front of you in traffic. *(Bonus points for anonymity!)*

FORM DAILY GRATITUDE RITUALS

Some people say grace before meals, others send birthday texts or mail cards. Find a ritual that is meaningful to you and make it a part of each day's gratitude practice.

Michele D. Baker

APPENDIX A

This Year, I'm Going to Let Go of the People and Situations That Don't Serve Me
Inspired by an article by Brianna Wiest

"It is the hardest thing you will ever have to do, and it will also be the most important: stop giving your love to those who aren't ready to love you.

"Stop having hard conversations with people who don't want to change. Stop showing up for people who are indifferent about your presence. Stop prioritizing people who make you an option. Stop loving people who aren't ready to love you.

"I know that your instinct is to do whatever you can to earn the good graces of everyone you can, but that is also the impulse that will rob you of your time, your energy and your sanity."

Brianna Wiest (briannawiest.com)

I don't know about you, but I'm tired of trying to change myself to make others happy. I'm tired of trying to be thinner, stronger, prettier, smarter, more creative, and a better cook. I'm tired of believing that if I were (thinner, blonde, taller, had bigger breasts...) that I would be worthy of some wonderful man loving me. I'm tired of believing that I have to work hard 40 hours a week to make enough money to buy lots of clothes and furniture and a new car. I'm exhausted from thinking that because I don't have a huge 401(k) set aside for retirement, I'm a financial failure. I'm tired of trying to be friends with the "popular women" (who started out as the "popular girls" in high school) – I have nothing in common with them. I'm tired of being shown on television, and in the movies, and in magazines that because I am single and have no children that I am not a "real" woman.

I'm tired of keeping up with friends and acquaintances who only call me when they need something. I know each person is on his or her own path, but I believe we should enrich our own lives by being grateful for friends – and part of that gratitude is reaching out to say "Hello, I love you today." I'm fortunate to have friends across the globe, but only a very few take the time to keep the energy moving on a regular basis. If you're reading this, you're one of those people – and I LOVE YOU!

Beyond all that, I'm tired of being *tired*.

But I think I have found a way out. I'm going to stop believing all these self-destructive thoughts – for goodness sake, I have a team of celestial beings talking to me every day! This is where the doubt creeps in, you know. For all the times I wrote down their words and thought I understood, there was still this deep well of insecurity that kept me prisoner in a glass-walled room of my own design. And because the walls are clear, I could pretend they weren't there.

But it's exhausting trying to be perfect and trying to make people love me. There will always be someone who won't do what I want, or in some way won't live up to my expectations. So I make this vow: I hereby <u>give up</u> those unrealistic expectations of others and outdated ideas about myself; those lazy, ill-considered thought patterns in our 3D systems; those destructive, brain swirling rabbit trails that spiral you down right into the dirt.

From now on, if something makes me sad, I'll say "no" to it.

From now on, if I see something that feels wrong, I'll take another path.

From now on, if I don't feel nourished and loved by a person, I'll allow that relationship to take a back burner. As Wiest suggests, I will "stop loving people who aren't ready to love [me]."

Finally, I will remember that each piece of this magnificent life is merely another opportunity to add to the Akashic Records, and I set it up beforehand, with full knowledge of what I was doing. What a miracle!

APPENDIX B

Summary of **"How Gratitude Changes You and Your Brain: New research is starting to explore how gratitude works to improve our mental health"** by Joshua Brown & Joel Wong (June 6, 2017). *Article used with permission.*

Read the full article at https://greatergood.berkeley.edu/article/item/how_gratitude_changes_you_and_your_brain

The Question

Mental health professionals are asking: How can we help clients derive the greatest possible benefit from treatment in the shortest amount of time?

One answer: complement psychological counseling with additional activities that are not too taxing for clients but yield high results, including the practice of gratitude. Many studies over the past decade have found that people who consciously count their blessings tend to be happier and less depressed.

The problem is that most research studies on gratitude have been conducted with well-functioning people. Is gratitude beneficial for people who struggle with mental health concerns? *If yes, how?*

300 Students in 3 Groups

Research involved 300 adults, mostly college students who were seeking mental health counseling at a university. The majority struggled with depression and anxiety.

Participants in the study were randomly assigned into one of three groups. All three groups received counseling services. Group 1 was also instructed to write one letter of gratitude to another person each week for three weeks. Group 2 was asked to write about their deepest thoughts and feelings about negative experiences. Group 3 did not do any writing activity.

The Results

Compared with the participants who wrote about negative experiences or only received counseling, those who wrote gratitude letters reported significantly better mental health four weeks and 12 weeks after their writing exercise ended. This suggests that gratitude writing can be beneficial not just for healthy, well-adjusted individuals, but also for those who struggle with mental health concerns. In fact, it seems practicing gratitude on top of receiving psychological counseling carries greater benefits than counseling alone, even when that gratitude practice is brief.

4 Insights

And that's not all. When we dug deeper into our results, we found indications of how gratitude might work on our minds and bodies. While not definitive, here are four insights from our research suggesting what might be behind gratitude's psychological benefits:

A. Gratitude unshackles us from toxic emotions

First, by analyzing the words in each of the two writing groups, we were able to understand the mechanisms behind the mental health benefits of gratitude letter writing. We compared the percentage of positive emotion words, negative emotion words and "we" words (first-person plural words). Those in the gratitude writing group used a higher percentage of positive emotion words and "we" words, and a lower proportion of negative emotion words, than those in the other writing group.

However, people who used more positive emotion words and more "we" words in their gratitude letters didn't necessarily have better mental health later. It was only when people used fewer negative emotion words in their letters that they were significantly more likely to report better mental health. In fact, the lack of negative emotion words – not the abundance of positive words – showed the mental health gap between the gratitude writing group and the negative writing group.

Gratitude letter writing produces better mental health by shifting one's attention away from toxic emotions such as resentment and envy. When you write about how grateful you are to others and how much other people have blessed your life, it becomes considerably harder for you to ruminate on your negative experiences.

B. Gratitude helps even if you don't share it

Participants who were assigned to write gratitude letters *weren't required* to send their letters. In fact, only 23% of participants who wrote gratitude letters sent them. But those who didn't send their letters enjoyed the benefits of experiencing gratitude, nonetheless.

This suggests that the mental health benefit of writing gratitude letters is not entirely dependent on communicating that gratitude to another person.

So if you're thinking of writing a letter of gratitude to someone, but you're unsure whether you want that person to read the letter, write it anyway. You can decide later whether to send it (and we think it's often a good idea to do so). But the act of writing the letter can help you appreciate the people in your life and shift your focus away from negative feelings and thoughts.

C. Gratitude's benefits take time

The mental health benefits of gratitude writing did not emerge immediately, but gradually accrued over time. Individuals in the gratitude group reported better mental health four weeks after the writing activities, and the difference became even larger 12 weeks after the writing activities.

D. Gratitude has lasting effects on the brain

About three months after the sessions began, we took some of the people who wrote gratitude letters and compared them with those who didn't do any writing. We wanted to know if their brains were processing information differently.

We used an fMRI scanner to measure brain activity while people from each group did a "pay it forward" task. Individuals were regularly given a small amount of money by a "benefactor." This benefactor only asked that they pass the money on to someone if they felt grateful. Our participants decided how much of the money, if any, to pass on to a worthy cause.

We wanted to distinguish donations motivated by *gratitude* from donations driven by other motivations (such as guilt or obligation). We asked the participants to rate how grateful they felt toward the benefactor, how much they wanted to help the worthy cause, and how guilty they would feel if they didn't help.

Across the participants, when people felt more grateful, their brain activity was distinct from brain activity related to guilt and the obligation to help a cause. We found that when people who are generally more grateful gave more money to a cause, they showed greater neural sensitivity in the medial prefrontal cortex, a brain area associated with learning and decision making. This suggests that people who are more grateful are also more attentive to how they express gratitude.

When we compared Group 1 (gratitude letter writers) with Group 3 (no writing), Group 1 showed greater activation in the medial prefrontal cortex when they experienced gratitude in the fMRI scanner. This is striking as this effect was found three months after the letter writing began. This indicates that simply expressing gratitude may have lasting effects on the brain and that practicing gratitude may help train the brain to be more sensitive to the experience of gratitude down the line, which could contribute to improved mental health over time.

The Bottom Line

Though preliminary, our research suggests that writing gratitude letters may be helpful for people seeking counseling services and explains what is behind gratitude's psychological benefits. At a time when many mental health professionals are feeling crunched, we hope that this research can point them and their clients toward an effective and beneficial tool.

Sources:
https://www.tandfonline.com/doi/abs/10.1080/10503307.2016.1169332
https://www.sciencedirect.com/science/article/abs/pii/S1053811915011532

APPENDIX C

Five Element Theory
From www.MyHealingPartner.com

What are the Five Elements?

The Five Element theory describes **wood, fire, earth, metal,** and **water** as the basic elements of the material world. In Chinese medicine, elements help us understand the patient and their personality. It also helps determine an effective treatment plan for medical problems.

The 5 Elements are continually evolving and changing within you, and some elements become stronger and more dominant at different stages in life. The five elements help explain physiology and pathology within the body. Each element has unique characteristics and are associated with season, weather, color, personality type, and symptoms/disease states.

	Wood	Fire	Earth	Metal	Water
Personality	Athletic, energetic, adventurous	Passionate, creative, authoritative	Nurturing, generous, caregiving	Meticulous, honest, responsible	Wise, reflective, private
Possible issues	Orthopedic, TMJ, migraines, ADD/ADHD	Insomnia, high blood pressure, chest pains, headaches	Abdominal issues, hormone problems	Constipation, lung & skin issues, allergies	Back pain, knee pain, kidney and bladder infections
Organs	Liver, Gallbladder	Heart, small intestine	Spleen, stomach	Lung, large intestine	Kidney, bladder
Season	Spring	Summer	Late summer/ Harvest	Autumn	Winter
Weather	Wind	Heat	Damp	Dry	Cold
Direction	East	South	Center	West	North
Emotion	Anger	Joy	Worry	Grief	Fear
Color	Blue, green	Red	Yellow	White	Black, dark blue
Taste	Sour	Bitter, burned	Sweet	Spicy	Salty
Sound	Shouting	Laughter	Singing	Weeping	Groaning
Sense organ	Eye	Tongue	Mouth, lips	Nose	Ear
Sensation	Vision	Taste	Touch	Smell	Hearing, balance

Body tissue	Tendons & sinews	Veins & arteries	Muscles, flesh	Skin	Bone, marrow, central nervous system

Cycles of Creation, Cycles of Destruction

The Elements are all connected. Wood feeds Fire, Fire makes Earth, Earth creates Metal, Metal holds Water, and Water nourishes Wood. Wood roots Earth, Earth dams Water, Water extinguishes Fire, Fire melts Metal, and Metal cuts Wood. Each element both controls and is controlled by another element. The system is connected, moving, and constantly in a process of balance. One element may manifest heavier within us than others. This is where we are strongest, yet most vulnerable.

The Meridians and Acupuncture

Meridians are invisible "rivers" of energy that run through the body in channels. Our life energy ("qi/ki/chi") flows along these meridians, and when it is blocked or disrupted pain, discomfort, and illness can occur. Acupuncture treatment involves transferring energy from one element to another creating balance again. There are 12 main meridians in Traditional Chinese Medicine, and each meridian is associated with a different body organ. Acupuncture needles target specific points on specific meridians, and this restores proper energy flow. (Acupressure on the corresponding points can also be helpful.)

As always, this information is meant as a starting point for your own research and discernment and isn't meant as medical advice. I encourage you to learn more about the fascinating world of Traditional Chinese Medicine—including massage and bodywork, tai chi, acupressure and acupuncture, reflexology, Shiatsu massage, herbal remedies, and more.

APPENDIX D

Mayan Calendar

The Mayan calendar called the Tzolkin (zol-KEEN) is the oldest of the Mayan calendar systems. Based on the growing season of maize (corn), the "count" is 260 days, roughly equivalent to a year in the Gregorian calendar. Each "week" is called a **Trecena** (truh-SEN-uh) and is made up of 13 tones (24-hour periods like days)—also called **Kin** (KEEN)—which begin at sunrise and last until the next sunrise. These days/tones/Kin make up one wheel and are numbered 1-13.

Each day has a certain unique "tone" or "flavor:"

"1" days – unity, beginning of new things
"2" days – duality, recognition of separation and desire to be reunited/rejoined
"3" days – action, communication, movement in 3 dimensions
"4" days – stability, setting parameters for game/relationship/work/project
"5" days – empowerment, networking, gathering needed materials
"6" days – responsiveness, negotiation, dynamic development
"7" days – reflection, ethics, purpose
"8" days – justice, harmony, and balance
"9" days – patience, perspective, larger picture
"10" days – manifestation into reality
"11" days – resolution, change, fitting in, adapting
"12" days – understanding, retrospection, accumulated experience
"13" days – ascend to the next level and begin again

A second, larger wheel interconnects with the Trecena wheel. This wheel is made up of 20 glyphs, also called "day signs." As with the days, each glyph has its own unique "flavor" or "tone."

Imix (ee-MEESH)/ **Crocodile** – open to new beginnings
Ik (EEK) / **Wind** – send communications of all kinds
Akbal (ahk-BAHL) / **Night** – spend time contemplating the stars
Kan (KAHN) / **Seed** – plant ideas, make new contacts, and reconnect to others
Chicchan (chick-CHAN) / **Serpent** – be flexible and fluid in all your dealings
Cimi (kee-ME)/ **Death or Transformer** – tie up all loose ends
Manik (mah-NEEK)/ **Deer** – be of service to others

Lamat (lah-MAHT)/ **Star** – ask for abundance in all relations

Muluc (moo-LOOK)/ **Offering** – offer appreciation for all creation

Oc (AWK)/ **Dog** – enjoy family and friends

Chuen (CHOO-in)/ **Monkey** à begin anything new in your life

Eb (EEB)/ **Road** – do some community service

Ben (BEN)/ **Reed** – bless or repair your house

Ix (EESH)/ **Jaguar** – commune with and give thanks for Mother Nature

Men (MAYN)/ **Eagle** – ascend to a higher/larger perspective

Cib (KEEB)/ **Wisdom** – sit on a rock and relax

Caban (ka-BAHN)/ **Earth** – give thanks to Mother Nature for her gifts

Etznab (ets-NAHB)/ **Flint** – spend time in reflection and introspection

Cauac (ka-WAHK)/ **Storm** – count your lessons as blessings and your enemies as angels

Ahau (ah-HOW)/ **Sun** – ask for the wisdom and continued honored memory of our ancestors

One "year" of 260 days is the time it takes for the 13 signs and 20 glyphs to rotate through one cycle. The first day of a new "year" is always 1-Imix/Crocodile. 2-Ik/Wind follows, then 3-Akbal/Night, and so on. On the 14th day we start a new Trecena/week, so we start over at 1 and the next day sign: 1-Ix/Jaguar. Then 2-Men/Eagle, 3-Cib/Wisdom. Because the wheels are not equal, it takes 260 days to cycle through and come back around to 1-Imix/Crocodile. (13 tones x 20 glyphs = 260 Kin = 1 year)

As Jag Stewart explains:

While people today in this modern age are relatively familiar with western astrology, the Maya had a different view of the relationship between ourselves and the cosmos that was not based on stars or planets, or anything physical. In western astrology, your birth sign and personality traits are fixed according to how the planets are aligned with the stars at the time of day that you were born, and then interpolated to provide some spiritual meaning for you to apply to your life.

There are 260 unique combinations of Tones and Glyphs. You were born on one of those 260 unique days. You have a "tone" and a "day sign" and that represents your true Mayan Calendar birth date, or to put it more succinctly, it represents the energetic qualities of the day that you departed from the uterine world to enter the Earth world and begin your life journey.

This brief information is meant to whet your appetite for more! There are countless books and videos available (just Google "Mayan Calendar" for millions of hits). My personal favorite is www.MayanMajix.com, which can give you lots more information about the Mayan Calendar: its origins, deeper meaning to Mayans, why it is of interest today, what happened since the Mayan calendar "ended" in 2012, and even applications to your daily life. Of special interest to me are the daily Tzolkin calendar, translating your birthday from the Gregorian into a Mayan birth date, and the "Articles" section. Happy reading!

GLOSSARY

3D human – *see Hue-man*

Akash, or Akashic Records – A compendium of thoughts, feelings, events, and emotions encoded within the non-physical astral plane; they contain the energetic records of all souls about their past lives, the present lives and possible future lives. Each soul has its own Akashic Records, like a series of "books," with each "book" representing one lifetime. Within that book/lifetime is recorded a person's entire history, including feelings, thoughts, decisions, lessons, outcomes, learnings and possibilities. The Hall (or Library) of the Akashic Records is where all souls' Akashic Records are stored energetically. In other words, the information is stored in the Akashic field (also called zero point field). The Akashic Records contain the collective wisdom of all sentient beings and are available as a resource to those beings. (adapted from Wikipedia and www.akashicrecordsofsouls.com)

Bi-location or bilocation – Celestial term for teleportation, the process of moving from one place to another instantaneously and without the use of technology (such as a car or airplane). Distinct from astral travel in that the corporeal body is also transported, not just the ethereal body.

C-RNA, Crystalline RNA, or C-RNA, is the new template that manifests changes in 5D and higher beings. In a spiritual sense, C-RNA co-creates the conscious aspects of the physical cells of the 5D and higher incarnate body. (Genes no longer control this function once the conversion to crystalline systems is completed.) *(see RNA)*

Channel - Channeling (or Channelling) is the process of communicating with any consciousness that is not in physical human form by allowing that consciousness to express itself through an individual, the Channeler [or in Michele's case, the "Vessel"]. Channeling usually refers to accessing higher knowledge to support spiritual growth and to gain greater clarity about one's life. It is a method used to access information from entities that are more evolved and can therefore enlighten us as we move through the evolution of consciousness and back to Source. (adapted from www.spiritlibrary.com)

Divine Feminine – Represents the connection to the part of your consciousness responsible for inward retrospection, nurture, intuition and empathy, regardless of your gender; the aspect of the self associated with creation, intuition, community, sensuality ("felt" sense rather than "thinking" sense), and collaboration. (adapted from www. SuzanneKingsbury.net)

Divine Masculine – Regardless of your gender, represents the connection to the part of your consciousness responsible for outward direction, logical action toward a goal, thinking, and making judgments about situations and consequences. It is the aspect of self associated with thinking, competition, calculation and rationality.

Draconians – Sentient humanoid reptilian beings usually associated with the star system Draco. Green, blue, gray/brown skin with scales. Very high intelligence, but below-average emotional responses. (adapated from www.Gaia.com)

Energy – Literal translation is "air" or "breath;" concept is known in nearly every ancient culture and is widely acknowledged in Eastern countries. This energy is the "life force" which permeates the body and animates it; in Traditional Chinese Medicine, the "chi" is said to flow through specific meridians in the body, and manipulating these meridians can restore or improve health. Also called "qi" in Chinese languages; "gi" in Korea; "ki" or "chi" in Japan; "prana" in Hindu traditions; "mana" in Hawaiian cultures; "manitou" in the Native American cultures; "ruah" in Jewish culture; and "vital energy" in Western philosophy. (adapted from Wikipedia)

Frequency, *see vibration*

Gaia – The sentient being that is the Soul of the physical incarnation of planet Earth.

Galactic Council or Galactic Federation – The Galactic Federation of Worlds (or Galactic Council) is a large federation of civilizations from many different planets, galaxies and universes working together for the harmonious existence of all life. There is a galactic federation in each of the inhabited galaxies of our universe. These federations are part of the universal management structure much like field offices are part of the management structure for a large corporation. (adapted from www.NibiruanCouncil.com)

Hue-man – Celestial term for the ascended Beings we are becoming, as distinct from "humans," or "3D humans" who are still in the process of ascension.

Interlife – A review and planning period between incarnations intended to allow Souls to assess lessons completed, lessons still to be learned, and to form contracts between all the "players" in a given lifetime.

Merkaba, or MerKaBa – Another name for one's Light Body. Part of full consciousness when spiritual, astral and physical bodies are integrated. The Merkaba allows Self to shrink to baseball size and to travel anywhere, instantly.

Reincarnation – Belief that after physical death, the same Soul returns in a different body to continue or expand on lessons or experiences of previous lifetimes.

RNA – According to science and medicine, Ribonucleic Acid (RNA) carries out a broad range of functions, from translating genetic information into the molecular machines and structures of the cell to regulating the activity of genes during development, cellular differentiation, and changing environments. *(See C-RNA)*

Sirians – Race of feline/leonine humanoids from the star system Sirius. These mathematically-minded scientists are master geneticists and engineers and are responsible for creating the original Earth human's physical vehicles (bodies).

Star beings – General term for sentient beings from other planets, galaxies or universes. (Examples: Sirians, Draconians, Andromedeans, etc.)

Synchronicity – A seemingly-magical (or seemingly-coincidental) coming together of people, places, and things to create a miraculous outcome.

Time out of time – Also called "time warps," time out of time is closer to an experience of true Time than what we perceive on a daily basis. True Time (capital T) is a series of endless Nows, a realm of pure sensation and experience. Example: You are reading an engrossing book, and look up to discover 2 hours have passed in the "blink of an eye."

Tribe – A group of individuals here on Earth to learn a lesson together; an organic, constantly-changing web of interconnected Souls. Your tribe is made up of those you choose to connect with to share your life, your triumphs and your challenges. May include friends, family, co-workers, pets, Nature, fellow congregants in a house of faith, etc.

Twin Flame – a special kind of Soul mate who is a lifelong partner, usually husband or wife (sometimes brother and sister or parent and child). Some traditions suggest that a Twin Flame is literally the "other half" or "matching partner" of your own Soul.

Vesica piscis – also called the "seed of life," it is two circles of equal diameter overlapping in such a way so that the center of each circle touches the edge of the other, creating two overlapping circles with a leaf-shaped center area. When 36 such circles overlap, they create the so-called "Flower of Life" pattern.

Vibration – the rate of speed at which something moves; the higher the vibration rate (or frequency), the faster something moves; the lower the vibration rate, the slower. As beings ascend, their frequency rises, until the molecules move apart enough for physical changes to occur (such as bi-location, spontaneous healing, etc.).

STUFF I LOVE (AKA ADDITIONAL RESOURCES)

BOOKS:

- "All For Love: The Transformative Power of Holding Space," by Matt Kahn
- "Channeled Messages from Deep Space," by Mike Dooley
- "Earth's Golden Age: Beyond 2012," by Suzie Ward
- "Find Your Why," by Simon Sinek
- "Illuminations for New Era: Understanding These Turbulent Times," by Suzie Ward
- "Jesus and the Lost Goddess: The Secret Teachings of the Original Christians," by Timothy Freke and Peter Gandy
- "The Laughing Jesus: Religious Lies and Gnostic Wisdom," by Timothy Freke and Peter Gandy
- "Life on Earth: Understanding Who We Are, How We Got Here, and What Might Lie Ahead," by Mike Dooley
- "Oneness," by Rasha
- "Path of Empowerment: Pleiadean Wisdom for a World in Chaos," by Barbara Marciniak
- "Perceptions of a Renegade Mind," by David Icke
- "Smile at Fear: Awakening the True Heart of Bravery," by Chogyam Trungpa
- "The Custodians," by Dolores Cannon
- "The Dot and the Line," by Norton Juster
- "The Nameless Man," by L.M. and Marianne Browning
- "The Tipping Point: How Little Things Can Make a Big Difference," by Malcolm Gladwell
- "The War of Art," by Steven Pressfield
- "The Way of Integrity: Finding the Path to Your True Self," by Martha Beck
- "Travels," by Michael Crichton
- Hay House library
- Homebound Publishers
- New World Library

WEBSITES:

- www.enlighteninglife.com (Jennifer Hoffman)
- www.AdventureInOneness.com (Rikka Zimmerman)
- www.marthabeck.com
- www.matthewbooks.com (Suzie Ward)
- www.drunvalo.net (Drunvalo Melchizedek's videos)
- www.lelon.us (Lelon Thompson, Intuitive Counselor)
- www.kryon.com
- www.inlightimes.com
- www.truedivinenature.com and videos (YouTube Channel: True Divine Nature)

MUSIC:

- Alasdair Fraser
- Amethystium
- ATB
- Blank and Jones
- Blue Stone
- Brule'
- Conjure One
- Daft Punk
- David Wahler
- Delerium
- Eastern Sun
- Enigma
- Friedemann
- Jens Gad
- Joey Fehrenbach
- Lindsey Stirling
- Mythos
- Nordlight
- Paul Oakenfold
- Paul Speer and David Lanz
- Peter Buffett
- Ralf Illenberger
- Ryan Farish
- Schiller
- Tangerine Dream
- Trapezoid
- Tycho
- Ulrich Schnauss
- Vangelis
- The Wingmakers

ACKNOWLEDGMENTS

Sincere thanks the many people who helped me write this book and who contributed edits and suggestions, including Dr. Julie Suman, Mrs. Lynne Creager and Dr. Fran Baker. I love you all!

Special Thanks

To my mother, Dr. Fran Baker, my strongest advocate since Day One. And to my father, Dr. John Baker and stepmother Dr. Susan Foster, who are now officially part of my Celestial Team.

To Dr. Joe Muscolino, who told me years ago the only thing I ever needed to know to fulfill this path: "Writers _write_. So, get up every day and just do it!"

To Mike Dooley, who read my book and took the time to comment on Amazon (a powerful author and very nice guy)

INDEX

Symbols